The Hunting Spirit

Quotes

"With his charm, wit and extraordinary ability to tell a good tale, Jerry captures the true essence of hunting. The stories remind us all that hunting is so much more than simply putting your tag on an animal. *The Hunting Spirit* is sure to adorn the mantels of hunting camps everywhere. **Darren Warner, *Outdoor Life* contributor**

"Jerry Lambert's new book *The Hunting Spirit* captures the hunter in all of us. His inspirational stories hit right to a hunters soul! This book is a must have for all outdoorsmen and women, you won't be able to put it down. Well done Jerry!" **Lane Walker, Author of the *Hometown Hunter Series.***

"In *The Hunting Spirit,* Jerry will leave you laughing, crying and learning something all at the same time." **Tracy Breen, Outdoor Writer**

"*The Hunting Spirit* is the second book from well-known Michigan storyteller Jerry Lambert. Reading these amazing stories immerses the reader in the essence of the hunt. It is no longer the kill but the moments that are most important to each hunter that Lambert captures. This is a must read for any hunter who dreams about big bucks, long beards or faraway hunting adventures." **Brian Miller, Outdoor Writer**

The Hunting Spirit

Hunting stories filled with inspiration and humor

Jerry Lambert

Big Mac Publishers, Kingston, TN 37763
Printed and bound in the United States of America

Author: Jerry Lambert
Editor: Connie Crofoot
All photos except where noted: Copyright © 2013 Jerry Lambert
Cover Illustration / Design: Sharie Schnell
Formatting: Michelle Lambert

Library of Congress Control Number: 2013949401

Library of Congress subject headings suggestions:

1. GV191.2-200.66   Outdoor life - Outdoor recreation
2. SK650-664   Wildlife-related recreation
3. SK295-305   Big game
4. GV200.4-200.56   Orienteering. Wilderness survival
5. SK40-268   By country - Africa

BIASC / BASIC Classification Suggestions:

1.   SPO022000 SPORTS & RECREATION / Hunting
2.   REL012040 Religion / Christian Life / Inspirational
3.   SPO030000 SPORTS & RECREATION / Outdoor Skills
4.   SEL021000 SELF-HELP / Motivational & Inspirational
5.   BIO023000 BIOGRAPHY & AUTOBIOGRAPHY / Adventurers & Explorers

ISBN-13 for Black and White Version: 978-1-937355-02-9   V: 1.0
ISBN-13 for Color Version: 978-1-937355-06-7   V: 1.0
ISBN-13 for eBook: 978-1-937355-03-6

To purchase additional copies of *The Hunting Spirit* or to learn more about the author go to his website: http://www.jerrylambertoutdoors.com There is also a Facebook page for *The Hunting Spirit* as well as for *Trophy White Tales* another terrific book by Jerry.

Big Mac Publisher Book Titles may be purchased in bulk at great discounts. Contact Jerry or go to Big Mac Publisher's website. www.bigmacpublishers.com

Big Mac Publishers, Kingston, TN 37763
Printed and bound in the United States of America

Table of Contents

Introduction: Into the Wild

The hunting spirit lives within the hearts of sportsmen and sportswomen around the world. It has existed since the beginning of time when God gave man dominion over the animals. The pursuit of wild game has a mystical aura that captivates the hearts of those of us who choose to take part in this time-honored activity. We possess a strong desire to be in nature and yearn to experience the sights, sounds and smells of God's glorious creation. We thrive on the suspense and anticipation that hunting offers. There is a lure that goes beyond the kill. There is appreciation for the land, the animal, and the chase.

Hunting and storytelling walk hand in hand. Fireside conversations and campfire tales are a traditional part of the sporting life. In September of 2011, I released my first book, *Trophy White Tales: A classic collection of campfire stories about North America's #1 game animal – the Whitetail deer*. This book quickly became an Amazon Bestseller in the hunting category and spent most of 2012 as the #1 Top-Rated Hunting Kindle book based on customer reviews.

The Hunting Spirit follows the same short-story format as *Trophy White Tales* but also includes stories about bear, turkey and African game. Once again, this book is a compilation of short stories that include fiction (Tall Tales) and real life adventures (Campfire Stories). Emphasis is to display the true spirit of hunting while maintaining the story format that was so popular in early outdoor literature. Honor is given to God (Meat Eater) and to our military (Hunt Camp). Hot Topics include conservation (Go Green), mentoring (To Whom Much is Given, Outdoor Ambassadors, Lessons Learned), and urban sprawl (New Country). Family traditions, camaraderie, camp life, inspiration and humor are spread throughout the stories, which fit the magazine format that hunters naturally crave. Turn the page and let your adventurous mind travel outdoors *into the wild* that you love!

Tall Tales
(Outdoor Fiction)

The Hunting Spirit!

The sun makes its first appearance for the morning and the bright light brilliantly awakens the day. The reflective light makes the frost and snow sparkle, the dew shine and the creek water glisten. Warmth returns to my chilled body and songbirds start to sing.

To get to where I am, I've walked a dark trail illuminated by the moon and stars. The hair on the back of my neck stands up as I hear a coyote or wolf howling at the moon. I walk to a pre-determined location, which often consists of a perch in the trees or a seat on the ground where I conceal myself in a brushed-in hide.

My inner being experiences a strong feeling of anticipation. Wondering if my prey is near, keeps my senses on high alert. My ears strain to hear approaching game as their feet disturb the forest floor or the tall grasses of a fallow field or marsh. I also listen for the tell-tale gobble of a tom turkey, grunts from a rutting buck, the bugling of a bull elk or the cackling of a rooster pheasant.

My eyes scan my surroundings for any sign of movement or horizontal lines among the vertical trees and shrubs. Sometimes I am enjoying either the fresh green growth of spring or the splendid colors of autumn or the barren northern habitat during the wintering months. Sitting in God's creation brings me closer to Him. Psalm 46:10 says, "Be still, and know that I am God. I will be exalted among the nations, I will be exalted in the earth." I know God.

A cool breeze slaps me in the face. The fact that I am facing the wind is a calculated measure that I have taken to hide my scent which could reveal my presence to the strong powered noses of most wild game. Those mornings in which I am pursuing wild turkey are the one exception.

My weapon of choice will sometimes hang from a limb, be propped up next to a tree or sit across my lap. I have held various shotguns, one gifted to me by my father and another that I won with a five-dollar ticket at a Pheasants Forever banquet. Sometimes I am holding my bow which I've spent a small fortune on to adequately accessorize it into a consistent killing machine. Strapped to my belt or stashed in my backpack is a razor sharp knife. With this, I hope to use at the conclusion of my hunt to field dress the game so that the meat can be cooled.

A glint of antler, the sight of a bluish-white turkey head or a bear ghosting through the timber, moves my heart to instantaneously pump in a rapid beat. On ultra-still days, I fear that the approaching game will hear my heart beating and abruptly leave. When I press my cheek up against the stock of my rifle, I can feel my pulse beat. If I am gripping my bow, I nervously get into position trying to find the opportunity to draw my bow without being detected by these keen creatures. When I place the bow site pin or gun scope crosshairs on the targeted vitals, adrenaline pumps throughout my body. When I pull the trigger and the deadly projectile does its job, I have successfully become one with nature and had a hands-on role in gathering high-protein food for my family and myself.

Admiring the downed game by picking up the antlers and counting points, stroking the coat of a predator, or admiring the long beard and spurs of a turkey, highlights the day. Giving a prayer of thanks to the Creator blesses the event. Posing for pictures captures the memory. Sharing these thrills with family and friends develops bonds that are stronger than steel and last forever. Camaraderie with our fellow huntsmen and huntresses allows for practical jokes, good laughs and great memories. Life is not measured by minutes but by moments, and these yearly hunting adventures provide inspiration and fond memories.

Fresh air combined with the smell of gunpowder and fire roasted venison lets one know that they are indeed in a place that they always want to return to. Proud parents and happy children seem to make up a high number of participants. The passing down of heirlooms and traditions thrive as well.

Campfires around the globe ignite tall tales that invigorate the soul. These stories resonate with the allure of opening days, the quest for adventure and the thrill of participation. My spirit has soared in Africa, America and Canada. The hunting spirit is alive and well!

Photo by Lindsey Barry

Hunt Camp

Tex runs into Big Jim and declares, "*Hunt camp tonight, spread the word. We'll gather at sundown. I'll have the fire started.*"

Big Jim smiles and runs off to tell the others. Tex is one of those natural born leaders that men admire and women are drawn to. He exudes confidence and is one of those rare cats who is equally respected by his peers, subordinates and those of higher authority. A real man's man if you get my drift.

The sky is colored orange as the earth's star sets on the horizon. Everything is big in Texas and Tex honors his homeland with a giant bonfire that leaps toward the heavens. Big Jim arrives with four other men who share one common denominator, hunting. The men shake hands with

Tex and then grab a beverage out of the cooler packed with ice and cold drinks.

Standing 6'5" in his cowboy boots and cowboy hat, Tex pops the top of a cold one and the men follow suit. Raising his can high in the air, Tex proposes a toast. The men raise their drinks and Tex shouts out, "Here's to shooting straight and living large!" A loud shout rings out followed by a loud exclamation from Big Jim, "Oorah!" The group then follows up with a synchronized shout, "Oorah!"

Paul passes out venison jerky and starts off the night of storytelling by describing his favorite hunting grounds in Montana. Spot and stalk is Paul's preferred method of hunting the cagey mule deer which sport heavy headgear that reach high into the sky. Snow is a familiar companion along with his brother, Steve. The jerky came from a tall tined, western count, 5-point that Steve shot a couple weeks ago.

When Paul finishes his tale, Cajun hits a duck call that hangs around his neck and then starts in about his favorite hunt in the flooded timber of southern Louisiana. Listening to the man with the jet-black hair describe the bird-filled skies and the abundant shooting gets the men fired up. Itchy trigger fingers is a common theme among this gathering of twenty-year old males as Cajun paints a vivid mental picture.

While the group pictures numerous ducks falling from the sky and splashing into the drink, Tommy stands up and commands center stage. Tommy's head is topped off with a Stormy Kromer cap that is made in the Upper Peninsula of Michigan. "Hunting to me is cold nights in my grandfather's cabin which is warmed by a woodstove and listening to the wolves howling at the moon. Finding an elusive swamp buck deep in the thick wilderness of cedar, spruce and pine is the ultimate hunter's high. Two years ago I tracked a big-footed buck after a fresh snow and shot him later that afternoon. He wore a gnarled 8-point rack that now accompanies my grandfather and father's collection on the cabin walls."

Wearing a western shirt and vest sits the newest member of hunt camp. Dalton passes around a photo of a Colorado bull elk wearing a velvet-covered crown of antler. "I found this bull right before I had to come here. I was able to sneak to within thirty yards and get this photograph before the wind shifted and he faded back into the timber. John Denver hit the nail on the head when he sang about Rocky Mountain High. There is nothing finer than chasing big bulls high in the mountains. Hopefully, I'll return and find him again during the open season."

Jesse, wearing a bear claw necklace looked at Dalton's picture, agreed that it was a fine looking bull, and wished him future success. Tex threw more wood on the fire and Jesse began with his tale. "Two years ago, as a high school graduation present, my father took me to Alaska on a black bear hunt. If there was ever a place like heaven on earth, this would be it. The sights were breathtaking. On my fifth day there, I shot a massive bear that had been feeding on an abundant supply of blueberries. We cubed the meat and cooked it in the fat trimmed from the bruin. To this day, it is the finest meal that I have ever eaten. If God allowed us to relive any moment from our past, that hunt would be my choice."

Tex and Big Jim completed the night by telling of a hog hunt that they did together in Texas. Jim proudly displayed blood stains on a faded camouflage shirt that he was wearing which testified of the event. These two friends share a deep bond forged through real-life experiences. They command a tough unit of fighting men who proudly serve their country. These heroic soldiers are stationed in the Middle East but through the activity of *hunt camp,* their collective minds can travel to the destinations of their dreams.

Before their tour is over, one of the members of the *hunt camp* will not make it home. Personal effects will be sent back to waiting loved ones. Will it be a cowboy hat, duck call, camouflage shirt, Stormy Kromer hat, bear claw necklace or a western shirt with a picture of a majestic bull elk? As fate would have it, Dalton's grieving parents received a package at their Colorado home containing a western shirt, the elk picture and a folded flag.

Tex and Big Jim completed their tours in the Spring and met up the following Fall. They decided to honor their fallen comrade the only way they knew how. They traveled to the Rocky Mountains and looked for the elusive bull elk from the picture. They found him in the black timber that Dalton spoke so fondly of. That night Tex made another campfire and raised a toast in honor of Dalton. Oorah! As Big Jim and Tex drained their drinks, two very tough men cried.

To all our military men and women around the world fighting to protect our nation, we salute you! Oorah!

I Believe In MONSTERS!

The flames leap for the stars and reflect the reddened cheeks of Boy Scout Troop, 333. Hot dogs and s'mores fill the stomachs of the young campers. Thirteen year old Trace Bisel assumes the role of class clown and jokingly asks in mock terror, "Mr. Rio, are there monsters in these woods?"

Mr. Rio is usually pretty laid back but this question quickly turns his demeanor serious. He develops an intense look in his eyes and stares intently at the young boy until all is quiet except for the crackling of the fire.

The muscular grey-haired leader then makes individual eye contact with all of the boys by slowly scanning his audience. Once he has their full attention, he turns his gaze into the flames and the words spill off of his lips in a scary, yet mischievous tone.

"Oh sure, I could tell you about the escaped convict who is credited with the murder of that fisherman on Pickerel Lake. Or, I could tell you about the nutty professor who checked himself out of the loony bin and reportedly walks these woods at night armed with an axe, but you have heard those tales and you asked specifically about MONSTERS!"

The boys let out a few nervous laughs but fear has already started to take hold and the fire's heat seems uncomfortably hot.

Mr. Rio continues, "I'm here to tell you, there are most definitely monsters roaming these parts of the woods, and they love the night."

The leader lets these words hang in the air before continuing. "These monsters are very seldom seen but if you pay close attention to the forest, it will tell you that they are indeed here. These huge beasts will sometimes leave behind a footprint in the soft earth that is far bigger than all others. They will also sharpen their weapons on the trees causing intense shredding or even total destruction. This may sound like something out of the book of Revelation but their weapons grow out of their skulls with several large daggers projecting skyward. One of the monsters reportedly has daggers pointing towards the ground as well. Further evidence has revealed that these crazed creatures have maimed and even darker reports state that they have indeed, killed!"

Beads of sweat are now visible on some of the boy's foreheads. Little Johnny squeaks out a question, "Has anyone ever tried killing these monsters?"

"Indeed they have," retorts Mr. Rio "Each fall when the leaves fall to the ground and visibility is at its best, gunman take to the woods with the sole purpose of killing these monsters. But you've got to know, these creatures are very hard to kill. They ghost through the swamps and thick cover and stay hidden during the daylight hours. It is very hard to even see one let alone kill one. If one is actually seen, it is still hard to kill. They have mystical powers that make even grown men break out in a fever. For reasons unknown, the fever causes uncontrollable shaking and shaky hands do not make a good marksman."

Mr. Rio is now staring blankly into the fire so Trace asks him, "Mr. Rio, have you ever seen the monsters?"

Mr. Rio hangs his head for a moment, then looks back up, and says, "Yes, Trace, I have. Last year I was walking that high ridge where we ate lunch today, when I decided to take a break and sit on a big oak stump. While sitting there, I thought that I saw something move down in the swamp. I stared in that direction and just when I thought that my eyes were playing tricks on me, I saw it again. Eventually, I could make out the creature, and it was one of the monsters. He was huge; I'm talking gi-normous. I raised my gun as he climbed the hill. At this point, I realized that I had the fever. I was shaking badly and my aim was poor. I panicked and pulled the trigger. The monster then started running away from me with alarming speed, and I proceeded to empty my gun without one of my bullets hitting the beast."

Trace's eyes were as big as saucers as he blurted out, "How close did the monster get to you?"

Tears started running down Mr. Rio's face when he answered in a shaky voice, "Twenty-five yards, that beautiful monster buck was only twenty-five yards away from me and I missed. I still can't believe I missed."

The boys looked at each other in disbelief and watched as Mr. Rio walked to his tent and put himself to bed. The boys were quite pleased to learn that Mr. Rio's monster was only a deer. Their collective minds were scared witless just seconds before. Johnny looked at the others and said, "He'll be ok guys, my dad's a deer hunter and deer hunters get pretty worked up about big deer. I'm just glad there are no real monsters out here."

As the Boy Scout troop started to relax and roast some more marshmallows, a pack of coyotes lit up close by. The boys took out their Swiss-army knives and sharpened their marshmallow sticks. Then they did what any adolescent males would do, they got more Mountain Dews out of the cooler and prepared for a long night around the protection of the campfire. I believe in monsters, do you?

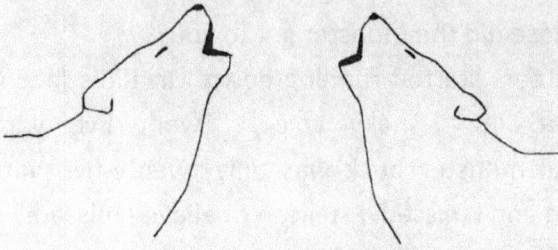

Two Alpha Dogs

One of my favorite sights in the whole wide world is the front gate of deer camp. This year, the familiar landmark is opened wide welcoming our anticipated arrival. Gorgeous Ponderosa Pines line our driveway, which winds back to a rustic log cabin. This north woods paradise was built by my grandfather's father in the fall of 1941. Since his passing, many moons ago, my grandpa Luke and his brother, Paul, have lorded over the manor. These two strong-minded siblings get along as well as fire and gasoline. They are both kind hearted old gents, except toward each other. If they adhered to the rule of, "don't say anything unless you have something positive to say", then I suppose they would never, ever speak to one another again.

When dad and I climb out of our rig, my Uncle Mike and cousin Mark pull in behind us. It is great to see them, and we are a chorus of smiles as we greet each other. Mark excitedly tells us that a bobcat ran out in front of them a few miles back and proceeds to tell us the whole story as we all make our way into the cabin. The smells of wood smoke and onions greet us at the door, and it is immediately obvious that grandpa Luke has prepared a kettle full of soup. Thick chunks of venison sit amongst a variety of garden planted vegetables. The warmth of the fireplace is rather pleasant and grandpa is awaiting us wearing his customary grin. Grandpa gives us all a firm handshake and asks the foolish question, "Are you hungry?"

We sure are and Mark and I quickly ladle up bowls of steaming hot soup. Dad asks grandpa where Uncle Paul is and grandpa mutters, "That old fool is at the lake trying to catch a mess of fish. It just tears him up that I already have shot a good buck with my bow. So, of course, that stubborn mule is trying to prove his worth through fishing, darn fool!"

Uncle Mike smirks and looks toward dad, then both exchange smiles and shake their heads. The two patriarchs are still feuding. Fortunately, they have nothing but love for everyone else.

After inhaling our lunch, we unload our gear. After that, Mark and I cut some more firewood and haul a few loads inside so that we won't have to waste too much of our precious hunting time. Our thoughts are continually reeling with mighty, big-racked bucks.

While splitting logs, Uncle Paul arrives with a bag full of perch fillets, and we know that we'll have a delicious supper as soon as we complete our camp chores. Just like grandpa Luke, Uncle Mike firmly shakes our hands and welcomes us *home.* The sun dips low behind the trees and a pack of wolves cut loose with their calls of the wild. Chills run up my spine whenever I hear their haunting cry. These hungry canines are starting their nightly hunt for food, and Mark and I are ready for another meal as well.

When we re-enter the cabin, the elderly statesmen are holding a heated discussion. Our human *wolfpack* has two alpha males and neither dog gives an inch. "Hey Julia Childs, hurry up with them fish. These boys have been working hard and they are hungry," barks Grandpa Luke.

Uncle Paul quickly retorts, "I bet they are. They probably didn't dare eat too much of that road-kill soup that you served earlier."

"Road kill my eye. You are just jealous because the last deer that you killed was back in the day when you still used a comb." snorted grandpa.

"I can take you by the cemetery plot of the last guy who thought he could talk to me like that if you like!" exclaimed a now riled Uncle Paul.

"Ah, don't get your panties in a bunch, you bear-breathed old coot," states grandpa in complete disgust.

These two feisty dogs would go on all night if you let them so dad wisely interrupted their assaultive banter and changed the topic to tomorrow's hunt. This seemed to work as a good-hearted discussion developed about the upcoming adventure. Snow was forecasted to start falling around midnight and called for three inches by daybreak. With this pleasant thought, we prepared for bed. Us young pups just had to brush our teeth while the two oldest dogs took an assortment of medicine as part of their nightly ritual.

Mark and I tossed and turned throughout most of

the night, dreaming about big-racked bucks that we hoped to shoot the following day. Around 3 a.m., I got up and stoked the fire adding a couple of logs into the fireplace to warm the now, cold cabin.

At 4:30 a.m., dad started frying eggs while I manned the toaster and Mark set the table. Breakfast went down fast and we eagerly prepared for the hunt. Grandpa chose to stay behind and prepare lunch. Uncle Paul was unusually quiet. Most years he would be the first one out the door but this year he took his time. I just thought that he was savoring the moment.

Dad and I lit down a path to the north. He had a spot about a half mile out and my spot was another quarter mile further north. Both of us faced the west, which was the predominant wind for our region.

It was a quiet, still morning and I saw one buck and five does, but they slipped steadily through the cover never presenting me with a good shot. Around 10 a.m., I heard two shots within a five minute period but wasn't sure from which direction they came. At 11:30 a.m., I met up with dad and we returned to the cabin. Dad told me that he saw the same six deer that I had seen and a spike horn that he let pass. We both concurred that it was a wonderful morning, and we were excited to see what had been shot.

Uncle Mike and Mark beat us back to the cabin and had an 8-point hanging from the buck pole. Mike shot the buck as it dogged a doe through the fresh snow. He was pretty excited and proud of his shot. Mike shot the big brute right behind the shoulders taking out both lungs. Dad asked him where the other shot hit and Mike responded that he had only shot once. He had also heard another shot but thought that it came from our direction. We assured him that it did not and quickly conclude that Uncle Paul must have shot.

It was now 12:30 p.m. and we decided that we had better go help Uncle Paul retrieve his deer, if in fact, it was he who shot. Grandpa quietly asked to go along and seemed rather concerned. Paul's stand was just off the logging road so we took the two four-wheel drive trucks. Grandpa rode with us and I saw him nervously tapping on his knee and we bumped down the trail. I couldn't figure out what was bothering him.

When we arrived at the stand, it was empty except for a spent, brass-shell casing. Tracks in the snow led from the ridge down into a clearing. The trail led us to a pool of blood. We then followed both the tracks from Uncle Paul and the deer, along with a steady stream of blood that was easily seen atop the white snow. The trail took us into a grove of pines. We soon found Uncle Paul sitting in the snow resting his back against the back of a big-racked buck. Us boys counted out twelve long tines, six per side.

Grandpa knelt down and asked Paul if he was all right? Paul shook his head no and clutched at his chest. Jubilation quickly turned to concern. Fortunately, we had brought a sled to drag the buck, so instead, we carefully positioned Uncle Paul on it. We then *slid* him back to the truck. Getting Paul uphill was not easy but adrenalin played an integral part in us achieving our dire goal. We then made a run for the hospital and placed a call to 911. An ambulance met us half way en route and was able to start much needed treatment.

Waiting in the hospital for results was a mind-numbing task. Grandpa left the room and was gone for quite a while. After some time, dad went in search of him and found him praying in the chapel. Soon we were all in there praying alongside grandpa. A nurse found us and escorted grandpa to Paul's room. The doctors performed a heart cath and found that one of the main arteries leading to the heart had a 90 % blockage. Uncle Paul needed sleep but thankfully, he was going to be ok. Wouldn't you know it, he had to stay in the hospital another three days and grandpa never left his side.

On the fourth day, grandpa and Uncle Paul came back to camp. We lowered Paul's great deer from the buck pole and took a few pictures. After all, the tall tined, 12-pointer was the biggest buck ever taken at our northern paradise. Paul handed his own camera to dad and requested that another picture be taken. Uncle Paul then asked grandpa to help him hold the rack up high and dad took what turned out to be the best picture of the day.

That hunt took place twenty-five years ago. Two things died that day, a great buck and a long running feud. Uncle Paul lived another fifteen years and grandpa passed on just a couple of months after the funeral. These two warriors stood tall till their dying days. Their picture now sits in the center of the fireplace mantel with these words carved in the frame, "*Two Alpha Dogs Lead this Pack.*" Uncle Paul's 12-point rack hangs from the fieldstone above the mantel.

The rest of us still hunt the northern camp, and we

are now accompanied by my son, Luke, and Mark's son, Paul. The front gate remains a welcoming sight. Two metal wolf silhouettes have been welded to the landmark. The two howling dogs face each other and remind us of two great men. When the boys finish cutting and splitting wood, I will once again tell them about Grandpa Luke and Uncle Paul as we eat bowls of venison soup and fresh perch fillets. The cry of the wild is alive and well!

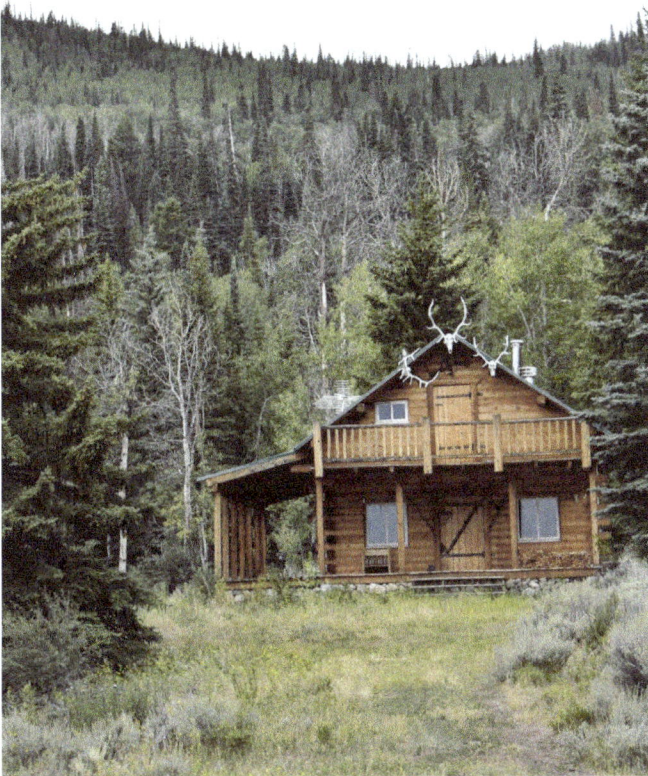

The Makeover

Saturday mornings are always a busy time at Shawn's Shortstop Barbershop and today was no exception. Shawn was busy finishing up a Mohawk haircut for one of the local high school football players and Scott was shaving the head of a swimmer who came in with long sun-bleached surfer hair. Sports and girls were the topics of the day until boisterous Bob burst through the door and loudly exclaimed, "Happy Birthday to me. You all aren't going to believe what my wife has done for my birthday!"

"Did she get you that new bow that you have been hinting about for the last year," asked Shawn?

"No, it is even better than that," retorted a very excited birthday boy.

Scott looked on with obvious doubt and asked, "What could possibly be better than a new bow?"

Bob puffed out his chest and proudly declared, "Bonnie has contacted a popular television show and they are going to do a Deer Camp Makeover!"

Well up until this point, Marshall had sat quietly reading the current issue of *Woods & Water News*, but any mention of deer camp quickly aroused his attention so he naturally jumped into the conversation and asked, "What in tar-nation is a makeover?"

Swimmer boy answered, "These makeover shows take something that is old, run-down and ugly and transforms them into something totally rad. You guys should make real good candidates."

Ignoring the obvious insult, Shawn's face breaks out into a big ole Texas grin and he enthusiastically says, "Wouldn't it be great if it was Toxey, Cuz and the Mossy Oak crew. They could plant some of that Bio-logic and improve our food-plots!"

Scott also gets caught up in the excitement and jumps in with, "Or maybe Realtree will send Jeff Foxworthy in with some of that Tecomate seed and we can steal all of the deer living on the neighbor's property too."

Marshall looked to be deep in thought and added, "Our lodge could definitely use some fixens, and we have definitely neglected some of its upkeep the last few years."

The Mohawked kid chuckled and said, "Lodge, what lodge? Are you referring to that run-down shack at your camp. That things so ugly the deer come onto your property just to laugh at it."

Well, the deer camp members wanted to fire off a retort but it is hard to argue when someone is right, so Shawn just slapped him upside the head and said, "Shut up fool." Swimmer boy laughed and Scott slapped him as well.

Bob was none too amused at being the butt of two high schooler's jokes but they were right, and the truth hurts so he said, "These two chuckleheads are right, so that is why I'm so excited. Well, that, and the fact that we are all going to be TV stars."

Mohawk chimed in, "Bob, you do have a good face for radio."

Bob smiled and said, "Thank you." The high school boys exchanged looks and started laughing hysterically.

The following Saturday, Bob meets the producer of a show called *Stevie Blade's Marvelous Makeovers*. Bob gives the producer a tour of camp. Special attention is given to the lodge, food plots and deer stands. The producer takes extensive notes, says that he finds the cabin to be in horrific shape and agrees that the camp is a prime candidate for their show. Before leaving he agrees to return in one week with the show's host, makeover staff, construction workers and production crew. Bob is riding cloud nine and can hardly wait.

Shawn, Scott, Marshall and Bob all arrive early on the day of the "big makeover." Naturally, they are all wearing their favorite camouflage caps, shirts and jackets. Their collective minds have been racing for two weeks and they were all ready for their 15 minutes of fame. Little did they know just how famous or infamous they would eventually become.

A long fleet of production and construction trucks arrives promptly at 7 a.m. Before the men even knew what was happening, the producer whisked them into a limo and took them away. The driver instructed the men that the make-over was going to be a surprise and that they were going to be treated to a good time while the construction crews worked.

The first stop was at a gun club where they were treated to a morning of skeet and trap shooting. Television cameras captured the excellent marksmen in action. At noon, they were once again traveling in the limousine and this time they were taken to the Lumberjack Steakhouse. Extra large, one and a half inch steaks were placed in front of the burly men and the camp members happily gorged themselves. While enjoying dessert, the men engaged in a spirited discussion about previous hunts and about how much better everything would be after the makeover magic was completed. Hunting from well-constructed deer stands over lush food plots and then returning to a warm refurbished lodge was the common dream.

The construction crews worked fast while the

anxious hunters waited to be returned to camp later that evening to see the new and improved Camp Whitetail. On the return trip to camp, the four men were blindfolded so that they would be *surprised* when the makeover was revealed.

With bright lights blazing and cameras rolling, the men were allowed to remove their blindfolds. Standing before them with a microphone in his hand was the host of *Marvelous Makeovers,* Stevie Blade. Stevie was wearing a coonskin cap, neon green jacket, pants that looked a lot like tights and suede boots. When the foursome saw this ridiculous looking creature standing before them, they instantly knew that they were in for an unpleasant *surprise.* Scott stared at Stevie and let out a loud disdainful, "Ugg." Surprisingly, Stevie responded with a girlish shrill and exclaimed, 'Why yes, I am wearing Ugg Boots but enough about me, look around you, doesn't everything just look m-a-r-v-e-l-o-u-s!"

The expressions on the men's faces registered shock and awe. Stevie pranced around the "new lodge" with camera crew in tow jabbering about the many f-a-b-u-l-o-u-s improvements. Everywhere the eye could see, there were scented candles and flowers. New shelves held various plants that made the walls look more like Wrigley Field than a hunting lodge. Stevie was talking in a theatrical narrative, "As the lead designer, I chose to keep the nature theme by adding plant and floral arrangements. I then added window treatments that complimented the overall color scheme of pastels, pulling colors from the various flowers. The antlers that were already on the walls made great hangers for potpourri baskets. Scented candles were added to further neutralize the prevalent smells that had developed over time and um...mismanaged upkeep."

The men stood speechless. In one day, their precious lodge had been transformed into a girly dollhouse and contaminated with enough scent to scare deer away for the next 10 years! Heck, the skunks had probably even left the region by now.

As if things couldn't get any worse, the men were escorted outside to show them the "improvements" that had been made to their property. The men's strategically placed tree-stands had been replaced by raised shantys. These would have been wonderful if Stevie and crew hadn't dolled them up like they did the main lodge. That, and the fact that they were painted chartreuse and mauve.

Stevie was told by his research staff that the hunters went to the stands before light, so he "kindly" had their footpaths lit up with solar lights to help guide them in the dark. The coup de grace was the fact that the food plot areas were converted to mini sports fields providing fitness recreation opportunities to these obviously out-of-shape camp members. Shawn's stand now overlooked a detailed soccer field, Scott's has a sand volleyball court, Marshall's has cement basketball courts and Bob's overlooked a picnic pavilion area.

Well, with the help of the new social medias, like Facebook and YouTube, the men became rather famous and or infamous as predicted. The barbershop quartet at first were laughed at unmercifully but people can laugh for only so long and then pity takes hold. As fate would have it, the

Camp Whitetail members would have the last laugh. Both Mossy Oak and Realtree heard about their terrible predicament and arranged for televised hunts on their respected properties. In addition, the city recreation department ended up buying Camp Whitetail to expand their sporting facilities and the camp members were able to take the proceeds of the sale to buy another camp with twice the amount of acreage and a truly rustic lodge. Some birthday presents just keep on giving!

Photo by Mike Persichini

Bartholomew

With the rain pouring down from the skies, ten year old Bart reluctantly came inside as directed by his mother. The wondering adventurer's curiosity took him into the attic of his grandparent's farmhouse. A large chest caught his eye. It looked like something pirates would use to stash gold coins and highjacked treasures. Without hesitation, Bart went to have a look inside.

A thick coat of dust covered the antique and quickly filled the air when Bart flung open the lid. Folded neatly inside was an old red and black checkered wool coat and matching cap. Under the outerwear was an assortment of papers including an old newspaper clipping about a local sheriff who shot the largest buck in the area for that year. At the very bottom of the pile was a framed picture of the bearded lawman wearing the checkered coat and cap. The man cradled a lever action rifle and was posed in front of a sagging buck pole that held a huge 10-point buck. The little man was staring at the old photograph when his mother knelt down beside him.

"Momma, who is this"? Bart asked his mother.

Smiling, Bart's mom responded, "That is your great-grandfather, Bartholomew, whom you were named after. Legend has it that he was a tough lawman who sought out adventure just like you."

Bart liked that his mom used the word tough to describe this man as well as himself. The youngster was drawn to the photograph and asked his mom if he could hang it in his room. Mom replied, "You will have to ask granddad, after all, this was his dad."

After a fantastic steak dinner, Bart respectfully approached his grandfather and asked if he could have the photograph. Grandpa was taken back at the sight of the picture and replied, "Oh my, I haven't seen this picture in years. Where did you find this?"

"It was up in the attic in a large chest underneath an old red and black coat," replied Bart.

Grandfather smiled and nodded, "Of course, I forgot about that old chest."

The old man stared at the picture and then stated, "I'll tell you what, you can have this picture if you agree to also accept the jacket and cap and another item that I have in the den."

Bart enthusiastically nodded his head *yes* and followed his grandpa into the den. They walked over to the gun cabinet and grandpa pulled out a vintage .30/30 and opened the lever action. The wood stock was chipped and showed wear but grandpa had the grain shining under a thick coat of lacquer and the blued steal was well preserved.

Grandpa held the gun out and stated, "This was my dad's .30/30. I think that your great grandfather would like you to carry this gun afield just like you have honorably carried his name, Bartholomew."

The little man proudly accepted the gifts and sincerely treasured them. He immediately started dreaming about one day getting his own trophy buck that would rival the one in the picture. Only time would tell.

Twenty years later, the thirty year old office manager is attempting to finish his work on a Friday afternoon. Within the last five minutes, he has sent ten e-mails including a very important one which has the fiscal year-end report attached to it. Next, Bart prepares a message that informs all incoming e-mails that he will be out of the office for the next two weeks. Bart leaves a similar message on his desk phone and then with a click of the mouse, he *shuts down* his computer. The anxious worker starts to pick up his briefcase but then smiles and lets it sit where it is. Hurrying towards the exit, Cathy attempts to ask a question but Bart cuts her off saying, "Whatever it is will have to wait, I'll see you in two weeks."

As Bart's left hand pushes open the exit door, his right hand snatches the tie from around his neck. Cool crisp autumn air splashes his face, and the warm sun shines brightly from a bluebird sky.

Bart climbs into the cab of his truck and fires up the horsepower. Within minutes, he is on the open road of the freeway heading due north and the transformation begins. The spirit of the wild soars within his soul, and the man's true self is ready to fly free.

As the sun descends behind the trees, Bart follows a long twisting two-track that takes him deep into the wilderness. An ancient trapper's cabin will serve as base camp for the next two weeks. Stepping through the doorway is like stepping back in time. Iron traps hang from nails in the log walls along with an impressive set of antlers from a large 10-point buck, the same antlers that are pictured on the buck that is in the photo from the attic.

The following morning, Bart slips on the red and black coat that fits him to a tee. He cradles the gifted .30/30 in the crook of his right arm and ambles out the door. It is a frosty morning and the stars shine bright. Bart rubs his chin and feels the fresh growth of his beard. A short jaunt takes him to the banks of the Cherokee River. Bart retrieves the canoe from under a large Norway spruce tree. Paddling upstream plunges him even further into the wilderness and away from his fellowman. Wild solitude is sought out and in addition, he is confident in finding a buck deep in the woods that has made it to old age. Bart beaches the canoe at the base of a ridge and follows a rocky trail to the top where the landscape consists of a thick forest of virgin timber.

The hunter has a grand view of a wooded valley. Bart chooses to sit there for the first couple of hours to re-acquaint himself to the ways of the wild. If nothing presents itself, he will then still-hunt the ridges after the sun melts the frost and wets the leaves.

When the first rays of sunlight filter through the trees, a dandy 8-point buck chases a doe into the valley, presenting a relatively easy fifty yard shot. Bart doesn't even raise his gun. It is too early and he truly believes that a true monarch can be found through diligence and patience.

Slowly, still-hunting the ridges, ten deer are spotted throughout the day including two other nice 8-pointers. When Bart drifts back down the river, he spots a beaver and immediately thinks that it would make a nice hat.

Over the next few days, a lot of ground is covered, and there is no sign of any other humans but lots of game. Bart has run the ridges and seen some dandy bucks. The desired brute that would rival that of his great-grandfather has yet to appear but many rubs have been spotted that indicate that this buck does indeed exist. Bart's beard is now full and his senses are highly tuned. He notices subtle changes with the sounds of the forest, and the hidden silhouettes of critters are observed before they flee to safety. Office manager Bart seems like a distant memory and the wild woodsman has fully emerged. The transformation is complete; Bart is now Bartholomew.

On the fourteenth day, big snowflakes fall from the sky. At mid-morning they quit falling but leave behind a blanket of white powder. The grizzled hunter is standing next to an old oak when he observes the slight twitch of an ear. This ear is attached to a bedded doe. Bartholomew's eyes are hidden underneath the bill of the red and black cap and scan the landscape looking for her possible suitor. Sure enough, there he is. A thick beamed rack carrying ten long tines adorns the massive buck. Bartholomew purses his lips and lets loose with a low whistle which brings the buck to his feet. The lacquered stock of the .30/30 fits snug against the hunters beard and the buck is quickly lined up in the sights. With a slight pull on the trigger, the rifle barks, abruptly quieting the woods of any future sound. Bartholomew works the lever but a second shot is not needed.

The successful hunter slowly approaches the buck, all the while seizing the moment. With the hustle and bustle of modern living, Bartholomew is thankful for the gift of hunting and the opportunity to slow down and interact with nature in the same manner that his forefathers did. A prayer of thanks is uttered toward the heavens, which seem extra real in the wilderness.

The hunter's woods-hardened legs march onward to the canoe with the prized trophy in tow. Loading the buck into the canoe is a daunting task, but it is successfully accomplished because it has to be. The can-do spirit of the wild makes things happen.

Bartholomew returns to work and, of course, there are pages of e-mails waiting along with another fifty voicemails. By mid-morning he has successfully tackled the task of prioritizing which messages need a reply and then his mind drifts back to the woods. His thoughts only last a minute before Cathy is knocking on the door. She politely asks, "How was your time off?"

Bart smiles, rubs his clean-shaven face and replies, "Refreshing and much needed! How have things been here?"

Without hesitation, Cathy launches into a highly-detailed narrative. Her voice soon fades out as Bartholomew mentally returns to the hardwood ridges. Getting re-adjusted to the office environment may take some time but he is in no hurry to fully do so. No hurry at all. Bartholomew is reluctant to allow Bart to return because the spirit of the wild continues to soar within his soul!

Samouflage's Turkey Tale

Spring means one thing to the group of men assembled at Indian Creek Gun & Archery and that is turkey hunting. Oh sure, they will speak of recent searches for morel mushrooms and shed antlers but them old long-beards is what really gets them fired up.

Store owner, J.J., is surrounded by three local archers whom he refers to as the three D's: Don, Dylan and Daryl. Don excitedly tells the group that the turkey that he has nicknamed *Boomer*, has lived another year because he heard the tom gobbling the previous morning during a scouting expedition. *Boomer* is an old bird that Don has steadily pursued the last two years with obviously no success. Don calls him *Boomer* because of his distinctive loud raspy gobbles.

Dylan enthusiastically chirps in, "Well, I heard *Houdini* last night so I get to hunt him for a third year as well. Dylan named his tom, *Houdini*, because of the way the bird disappears each morning after he flies down from the roost.

Not to be outdone, Daryl proclaims that *ZZ Top* is alive and well because he saw him walk across the road on his way to the gun & archery shop this morning. Of course, Daryl named this old bird *ZZ Top* because of the long thick beard that the tom has managed to sport for the last three seasons.

Out of curiosity, J.J. asks Daryl where *ZZ Top* crossed the road? Well now, Daryl is not known for being quick of thought and he blurts out the information before realizing that he is giving away his trophy bird's location, "Coon Hollow Road!"

Hearing this, Don nervously chuckles, scratches his chin and then asks, "Was that near the winding ridges that sit between Mud Lake and Snake-Bite Swamp?"

"It sure enough was. How did you know that?" asks Daryl.

"Well that's where I've been hunting *Boomer* the last two years," declares Don.

At this point, Dylan contorts his face which displays his confused state of mind and says, "I've been hunting *Houdini* on those same ridges the last two years. That's amazing that all three of us have old birds living in the same area!"

As the three-D's stand dazed and confused, J.J., begins chuckling to himself but the chuckles quickly turn into outright, full-belly laughs. Somehow in his hysteria, J.J. manages to blurt out, "You mean to tell me that you three idiots have been hunting the same bird for two years and that not only did you all fail to shoot him but you didn't even know that you were all after the same bird?"

Daryl, who is still rather confused, asks, "Are you saying that *ZZ Top, Boomer* and *Houdini,* our long-time nemesis, are the very same bird?"

Don hangs his head and mutters, "It sure enough looks like it!"

"Well, look at it this way. That old tom is one worthy adversary if he has outwitted all three of you for the last two years. Unfortunately, none of you guys are going to shoot him this year either so you better start scouting and find new birds to hunt," declares J.J.

"Now just wait a minute, what do you mean none of us three will get the old bird?" asks Dylan. "I suppose that you think that you are going to sneak upon him and ambush him now that you know where he is."

"No, I'm not going to hunt your bird but Sam is. He just told me that he is going to shoot a trophy tom on those very ridges that you all have been hunting," asserts J.J.

"Sam, are you referring to Samouflage, aka, Master of Disguise?" wonders Daryl.

"The one and only," retorts J.J.

Now Samouflage is a living legend in this part of the country. His amazing ability to blend into any environment and take trophy game is well documented in these parts. Just last fall, Ol' Sam took an ultra-wide buck right out from under the three D's so the men were not pleased to learn that they may miss out on another trophy at the expense of the master hunter.

Don's eyes started cautiously scanning the store as he spoke, "You mean to tell me that crafty son of a gun is hiding in plain sight right here in the store and he just told you that he is going to shoot OUR bird?"

The other two members of the three D's start scanning around the store wondering how Samouflage has disguised himself this time. All three of the D's eye the new life-size bear mount with great suspicion.

J.J. breaks their concentration by barking, "No, you idiots, Sam just e-mailed me."

Undaunted, Dylan pokes at the bear and asks, "Where did this bear come from? It wasn't here last weekend."

J.J. smiles and says, "Sam brought it in this morning asking me if he could keep it here for a while. I said 'sure', after all you don't see too many cinnamon-colored black bears and he is a dandy."

Dylan continues his inspection of the bear when J.J. adds salt to the wound. "By the way, you see that empty spot on the wall next to the bear? I told Sam that he could display the fan and beard there once he kills that ridge-running turkey that has given you all the slip."

Don quickly retorts, "You're right about that bird dying this year but he'll be wearing one of our tags, not Sam's, and you can take that to the bank." With that being said the three D's storm out of the shop to go formulate a plan.

The night before opening morning, the three D's successfully roosted their long-time adversary who is perched high in a big maple tree that sits along the edge of Mud Lake. The game plan is to surround the tree. There are only three directions that the big tom can fly down to and one of the D's will be waiting. Sweet dreams entertained the men throughout the night.

Opening morning the men are all at their pre-planned ambush sites an hour before first light. A night owl fills the still air with a loud hoot and *Boomer/Houdini/ZZ Top* lets loose with his distinctive gobble. The three D's licked their lips anticipating the sweet taste of grilled wild turkey and even sweeter success.

Shortly after first light, while Don sits tight beside a heavy oak tree, he hears an animal approaching from behind him. He slowly peaks around the tree and sees a big bear staring angrily at him. When the big bruin rises up on his hind feet, he lets out a menacing growl. Five shot turkey load is not adequate fire power against the large bear so Don quickly gets up and hightails it to the safety of his truck.

Within twenty minutes, Don is reunited with both Dylan and Daryl as they also sought security at the truck after having their own encounters with the ferocious bear. Daryl is the last to arrive and while he speaks of his scary encounter with the bear, he is interrupted by turkey talk coming from high on the ridge.

A feisty hen is having a lively discussion with one loud, boisterous gobbler. They banter back and forth for a full two minutes until a loud shotgun blast silences the woods. Even though none of the three D's would ever be classified as quick of thought, it didn't take a genius to figure out what had just happened. Samouflage had done whooped them again!

As expected, the three D's return to the archery shop and share their experience with J.J. The adrenalin is flowing as they recount the tall tale about the menacing bear running them off the ridge. J.J. takes it all in but finds it odd that a rogue bear would scare all three of the D's but not bother Sam who is obviously sharing the ridge with them. After a brief period of silence, Daryl speaks up and says, "That was one angry bear. His eyes were as red as his furry coat!"

J.J. jerks his head around towards Daryl and retorts, "You're telling me that the bear that ran you off those ridges was a rare cinnamon-colored bear?"

"That's right! He looked just like that one over there," declares Dylan who points towards a now empty spot in the shop.

Don asked the obvious, "J.J. where's the bear?"

J.J. smirks and replies, "Oh, he walked out of here right after you fellows left the other day. I told you Sam brought the bear in but I didn't think it would be right to tell you that Sam was the bear. He was very grateful to you boys coming in here and telling him the exact location of a trophy long-beard."

"But you told us that Sam e-mailed you that he was going to kill our turkey. You lied," cried Daryl.

"He did e-mail me; it was quite funny watching a bear work a smart phone while your backs were turned. Sam never ceases to amaze me," said J.J.

Once again, the legendary Samouflage performed his magic and got the biggest trophy of the season. As promised, Sam brought in the fan and the thick eleven-inch beard from the trophy tom formerly known as *Boomer/Houdini/ZZ Top* and put them on the wall. The legend lives on! What's next? Only time will tell!

Ace-High

Ring-necked pheasants flush from under the feet of the black stallion, followed by two blasts from a double barrel shotgun. Two roosters fall from the sky and Gabe Tackett dismounts to collect his bounty. This scene is repeated five more times on the western prairie, giving the weathered warrior an even dozen.

Gabe puts the birds into two sacks that are tied onto the horn of his smoothly worn saddle. A tail-wind pushes the rugged cowboy back to the cattle drive which is currently camped along a wide shallow river. Gabe's mouth waters at the thought of the roasted birds. Gomez will season them just right and create a tasty treat; this he knows.

Later that evening, Gabe sits at the campfire and enjoys a cup of coffee. Trail boss, Ty Colter, sits on the other side of the fire. The other men give these two rugged, ace-high, cowboys a wide berth. Respect is earned in the West, not given and these two have earned it in spades. Their legendary deeds could fill volumes of the ten-cent booklets that marvel the talents of much lesser men.

Ty looks at Gabe and grins, "Fire-roasted pheasant, it don't get no finer."

"I thought some white meat would be a good change of pace," replied Gabe.

The men spend the next several minutes sitting in silence savoring the occasion. Cowhand Hank fills the air with the sound of his brass harmonica.

When Ty speaks again, a serious tone resonates in his voice, "I'll need you to scout and find our next water tomorrow, but be careful. I have a feeling down in my gut that trouble is awaiting. Do you want me to send Hank out with you?"

Gabe drains his cup, stares at the stars and says, "I prefer to go alone, I'll be out well before light."

It is as Ty expected it but as boss, he had to voice his concern. He could count on one hand the number of times that his gut feelings were actually wrong. He hopes that this will be one of those times, but he highly doubts it.

Sitting at Hank's campfire is a young buck named Luke and a wise old timer named Sam. Luke's been pondering for a while so he decides to finally ask, "What's Gabe's story? Boss sure favors him. Why is that?"

Sam looks at the green-horn and blurts out, "Let me give you some advice boy. Be careful before you pry into another man's business while out here. You could find yourself killed. I can tell you Gabe's story because it ain't a secret. His mother named him after the arch angel, Gabrielle. Gabe was a top lawman in Tennessee. Folks in those parts loved him and even wanted to make him the next governor but Gabe wanted no part of that. He said that it would cut into his hunting and fishing time. As a lawman, he sawed down a half dozen outlaws with those cat-quick reflexes. He was and for that matter, still is, highly respected. Gabe's heart hardened when the fever took his wife and son. Ten days after his wife's burial, Gabe turned in his badge, mounted up and came out West. Boy, you will probably never again ride with men with such a strong pedigree as Gabe Tackett and Ty Colter. If you are smart, you need to watch them and learn."

Gabe's worn, dusty boots hit the stirrups early the next morning. Strapped into the scabbard is a .44 caliber Henry rifle with a 16-round magazine. Holstered on his side is a Colt .44 revolver.

When the rising sun made its first appearance, Gabe was five miles from camp. The black stallion was hidden under a grove of sycamores. Gabe had climbed a rock outcropping that gave him a view of the stretching valley floor. From this lofty perch, he would sit and observe. There were no fresh tracks of fellow travelers but these parts of the West were crawling with rustlers, killers and thieves. A wolverine scampered along some rocks below. He had heard of this vicious animal but this was his first time actually seeing one. A half hour later, a mountain lion took the same path as the wolverine. The area must be rich with wild-game for this kind of predator activity. Gabe kept a watchful eye on a grove of cottonwoods that probably held the desired water source.

A mule deer buck casually grazed in a grassy meadow wearing a wide antlered rack that easily exceeded anything else that the hunter had ever shot. Normally, Gabe didn't shoot game this far away from the cook. Gunfire would alert anybody within hearing range of his presence and that would not be a good thing, considering that he is alone. However, this buck was exceptional. The antlers were in velvet, which made them look even bigger. From a prone position, Gabe placed the fat muley into the sights of the Henry rifle and with the pull of the trigger, the barrel spit fire. The buck hunched up and ran into a cluster of pines.

Gabe left his lofty perch and descended down into the pines. Slowly working the blood-trail, the grizzled hunter found the big buck lying on the bank of a small stream. Good memories from his hunts in the Tennessee mountains reeled through his mind. He specifically recalled shooting a wide buck that carried ten comparable tines. He took the tines and crafted them into silverware handles as well as for the knife that is sheaved on his belt. As the thought of his wife bringing the venison roast to the table crossed his mind, his ears took in the sound of horses walking the stream.

Gabe removed the tie down from his side-arm and cocked the hammer of his rifle. Four riders were approaching and they looked like trouble. Before Gabe could seek cover, they were upon him. Gabe cussed himself for foolishly letting these rough-riders close in on him. The excitement of the hunt dulled his common sense, and now he was in a predicament that only he could solve.

A heavy set man sitting on a black and white mare grinned mischievously and said, "Howdy friend, what do you got there? Looks like a load of venison. Care to share?"

Gabe recognized the man; it was Walt Lilly. Walt and his companions were wanted for the murder of a homestead family. A ten year old boy survived their ambush and slaughter by hiding high up a pine tree. The kid easily described the overweight scoundrel to the Sheriff. Walt had a distinctive limp and red birthmark on his neck that grew up into his right cheek. This obviously riled Gabe who lost his own family and his sympathies were with the young boy.

"This venison is for the men working the cattle drive," Gabe sternly replied.

Walt and his crew started laughing before Walt said, "Your cattle drive is still some miles back, and me and the boys are hungry right now."

Gabe raised his rifle, aimed it at the fat man's belly, and spoke deliberately and slowly, "I know who you are and I know what you did. Now I need you four to slowly undo your belts and let those side-arms fall to the ground."

A lean man wearing a red bandana around his neck glared back and declared, "There is only one of you and four of us. You realize you're going to die today, don't ya?"

Gabe didn't flinch and retorted, "We're all going to die someday, but if you don't do what I tell ya, then you and the fat man will be dead within the next few seconds."

Quick tempered, the lean fellow reached for his gun. As he did this, Gabe shot Walt in the chest and then peppered the initiator with two bullets toppling him from his horse to a quick death. The other two riders were taken back by the quick exchange and while one of them froze in place the other fumbled for his gun. Gabe shot the fumbler in the shoulder and followed up with a shot through the heart. By this time, the fourth fellow had drawn his gun and shot Gabe in the shoulder spinning him to the ground.

After hitting the turf, Gabe looked up to see the shooter fleeing down the creek. Gabe drew his pistol and took three quick shots. Two of them hit the rider in the back and like his outlaw hombres; his soul went straight to hell.

Gabe started tending to his wound and was pleased to find out that the bullet went straight through. The bullet severed a nerve and the pain was intense. Right before passing out, Gabe heard another horse approaching. Hopefully, this rider was a friend or this would be the end.

The following morning Gabe awakened to the smell of tenderloins cooking over the fire. Tending to the meat was Hank. Hank looked at him and simply said, "I thought that the smell of venison might bring you out of that deep sleep. That buck you shot is like no other."

Gabe attempted to rise but his shoulder was stiff and sore. Hank stopped him, "Whoa, don't you mess up my bandages. You need to rest right there. Let's get some food in you before you go attempting any movements."

Hank pulled some meat off and fed Gabe. The juicy protein tasted good and would be vital for recovery.

Hank continued to cook and while he roasted the meat over the fire, said, "Ty had me follow you. Ty's gut told him there would be trouble and he knows that his gut is never wrong. He also knew that you wouldn't want anyone to accompany you but shortly after first light, he told me to go find you. I was just approaching the valley when I heard the shooting. I saw that you got four of them. By the looks of the tracks, it looked like that was all there were. Is that correct?

Gabe nodded but fell back to sleep. While he recovered, Gabe's mind continued to return to his life in Tennessee. Images of his lovely wife and bright-eyed boy filled his mind.

The Good Book says that "it is appointed for all men to die" and Gabe's time came all too soon. Just when it looked like he was going to pull through, the wound became infected and a strong fever took hold. Gabe died one week after the shootout. Ty spoke a few words over his friend and then he led the men on down the trail. A wooden cross marks the grave of this brave western hunter. You can't miss it; Hank lashed the wide antlers from the mule deer buck to the cross.

The cowboy is now reunited with his family in a much better place. The legendary tale of Gabe killing Walt and his gang of ruthless outlaws continues to live on as the story is repeated time and time again by cowboys seated next to campfires all across the western plains. One cowboy who has told the story the most is named Luke, and he wears an antler-handled knife on his belt. Luke always finishes his account with, "I never rode with anyone finer. Gabe Tackett was Ace-High, and I will fight any man who says otherwise!"

To this day, there has never been a need for a fight. The Legend of Gabe Tackett lives in the hearts of all those who have helped in taming the wild, wild, West!

Photo by David Kenyon

Randy's Bear Cleansing Ceremony

Ed stokes the campfire and gives new life to the ashen timber that was still smoldering from the night before. Flames leap toward a bluebird sky and our woodland grill is ignited and ready for business. Chuck reaches into the cooler and pulls out a package of hot dogs that are now swimming in the cooler's icy water. It is the fifth day of bear camp and time for lunch. Today's menu is the same as yesterday's, fire-grilled hot dogs, chips, salsa and pop. Mountain Dew and Coke are the runaway favorites.

Ed inhales his first two dogs and is munching on a third when Chuck finishes his first one. Sleepy-eyed Pete rouses from his rack and prepares himself a plate. The tired threesome stare into the flames. Fortunately for them, they are tagged out and are hoping that the fourth member of their party, Randy, closes the deal tonight. Randy has already gone to his stand in hopes of seeing a bear that has been hitting his bait early in the afternoon.

Pete and Chuck shot their bears the night before and tracking and retrieving carried on late into the early morning hours. Chuck comments, "Man, I am glad that I got my bear yesterday. Sitting over that stinky bait was starting to turn my stomach."

Refueled, Ed's vigor returns. The giant man wipes the corner of his mouth with the back of his hand and then blurts out, "Speaking of stench, is it just me or does Randy flat out stink?"

Chuck's eyes bug out and he spits out a mouthful of pop. "Whoa, tell us how you really feel big guy."

Ed responds, "Don't get me wrong, he is a likeable enough guy, but he really, really stinks!"

Pete nods knowingly and adds, "There's no denying it, Randy's momma named him right because his is indeed rand."

"Has anyone seen him take a shower since we've been up here? I know I haven't," asserts the ever boisterous Ed.

"Now that you ask, I haven't either," adds Chuck with a bewildered look on his face.

"If he was a rock band, he would definitely be Grand Funk!" Ed proudly proclaims.

The others chuckle and then Pete observes, "I can't help but notice that he must wear about a thousand dollars worth of the newest scent-concealing technology every time he goes afield. What good can that do when you smell like a walking landfill?"

"I hear ya. Anymore, you can't pick up an outdoor magazine without reading about the author's elaborate *scent- elimination strategy* and correct me if I'm wrong, I believe they all start with TAKING A SHOWER!" observes Chuck.

"Hear, Hear. I agree on both accounts. A: Randy is definitely due for a shower and B: The outdoor industry has gone completely overboard on this scent-elimination technology stuff. Fred Bear did pretty good without it. According to the experts, human hair carries the most scent and Ted Nugent wears a pony tail that reaches down to his tail-bone and yet he seems to be killing something every day of the year," said Ed.

"I totally agree. Last month I attended a seminar where this *pro-staffer* gave an all too in-depth, which translates into BORING speech about *his personal scent-control methods*. He blathered on, 'I am great because I shower before, during and after every hunt. I use blah blah shampoo, blah blah soap, blah blah dryer sheets, etc.'" Ironically, this mastermind wore more product in his hair that day than my wife does in an entire week. His cologne was thick enough to disguise the odor of a skunk," asserts Pete.

Ed looked at both Chuck and Pete and shook his head displaying a bewildered look, "I don't think it is any surprise that Randy is the only one who hasn't gotten a bear. He stinks and needs to take a shower, and one of you two guys need to tell him before we enclose ourselves in the truck for the long drive home."

Chuck retorts, "What do you mean, one of you two guys need to tell him, why not you?"

Ed displays a mischievous grin and states, "That should be obvious, I am way too blunt. I would probably hurt the poor guy's feelings."

Before the men could further protest, Randy rode up on his quad with a grin spreading ear to ear. Randy shut down the engine and took off his helmet. "I got the big one and dropped him in his tracks. The big boar knocked the bait barrel over and was standing broadside with his front leg stretched forward. I placed the bullet right through his heart and down he went."

The men were genuinely happy for their friend, and they eagerly went to help in the retrieval. When they arrived at the bait site, they were completely shocked. Lying beside the barrel was a true beast of a bear. It would later tip the scales at 535 pounds, dressed out. The outfitter showed up and took numerous photographs to use in future flyers and to place on his website.

Ed pulled the outfitter aside and asked him how he was able to get a bear to come into a bait site considering how bad Randy reeked with body odor. The outfitter smiled and replied, "I picked a bait site in which the bears can only enter from upwind. The tall rock outcropping behind the stand makes it impossible for bears to properly scent check the bait site. In addition, I had him use a climbing tree stand and instructed him to climb to a height of thirty feet, hence a successful hunt for your smelly friend."

Ed smirked and had a trick up his sleeve as well. Once the bear was properly dressed, skinned and quartered, Ed congratulated Randy for taking the trophy class bear and told him that we must thank the Great Spirit through a customary Native American cleansing ceremony. Ed then dipped his fingers into the bear's blood and marked Randy's cheeks, chin and forehead. Ed then filled a cup full of blood and poured it over Randy's head. When Ed finished, he jokingly said, "Now go and take a shower—that bear blood makes you stink."

Randy smiled and went to the shower room beaming with pride. Chuck and Pete smiled and were quite surprised at Ed's crafty maneuver. Chuck asked Ed, "Exactly from what tribe did you learn this bear cleansing ceremony?"

Ed quickly retorted, "A tribe with very clean warriors!"

New Country

Trent climbs the steps of the old farmhouse and walks onto the porch. His cowboy boots clank on the floor boards. Trent is here to meet Mr. Amos Wilson. He opens the screen door to knock on the wooden door.

When the door opens, Trent is greeted kindly by a tall, grey-bearded man who stands about two inches taller than his six foot three height. Amos firmly shakes Trent's hand and welcomes him inside. Amos leads Trent through a front parlor room, on past the kitchen and into a great room located at the back of the house. Lining the walls of this room are a couple dozen mounted whitetail deer heads adorned with huge headgear. Almost all of them are extremely thick and tall tined. A couple of the bucks have spreads that range out past the golden twenty-inch benchmark.

Throughout Trent's youth, his father had regaled him with tall tales about the legendary Boone County hunter named Amos Wilson. Legend has it that Amos took the best buck in the county for about a ten-year period and would often share wild game with his neighbors in need. Trent is now a twenty three year old journalist who is fresh out of college. One of the first stories that the young reporter wanted to write was on the legendary life of the famed backwoodsman that his father had spoken of so highly.

Classic country music can be heard coming out of a vintage radio. Trent scans the collection of taxidermy and asks Amos which one was his first buck? The tall gentlemen points to a thick-beamed 10-pointer that sports very tall tines. With a glint in his eyes and a grin on his face, Amos proceeds to tell his tale. "I shot that big brute in 1970, the same year that Elvis sang *Kentucky Rain*. It was a rainy November morning when that buck followed a rub-line through the pine grove. I got a second buck out of there in 1971; that year Jerry Reed had a hit with his song about a gator poacher named *Amos Moses*. Unfortunately, the landowner let some loggers clear-cut those pines and stripped out all of the trees in the fence rows as well. That completely ruined it for deer hunting."

Trent points at an extremely wide-horned buck that was mounted in a sneak position. Amos takes a sip of his sweet tea and then proceeds to answer the younger man's gesture. "That one was shot in 1972, the same year that Waylon and Willie sang *Good Hearted Women*. I shot that buck on a widower's place, Ms. Rose. That kind lady died the following spring and her children parceled off the land. It is now the Rolling Hills subdivision."

Next came the absolute biggest buck in the room. This monster was a giant non-typical that carried 22 points. Amos chirps up, "I got that one on the property owned by an old Indian. Everybody called him Chief. We made a deal. I promised him all the meat off my first deer if I could hunt his property. That was in 1976, the year that Kenny Rogers sang *The Gambler*. Well, I took a gamble and entered this buck's bedding area and successfully managed to jump shoot him like you would a pheasant. Unfortunately, a casino now sits on the spot where this great warrior lived."

Amos then walks over to a black-faced buck with a gnarly 11-point rack. "This buck was shot in the swamp behind my house in 1980; the same year that the Charlie Daniels band came out with their hit, *The Legend of Wooley Swamp*. In 1981, I shot that 6x6 typical that is next to him while on an oak ridge that lies north of the swamp. That was the same year that the Oak Ridge Boys delivered their hit, *Fancy Free*."

Trent was collecting a lot of information for his article and receiving quite the history lesson in country music. He learned that Amos took his one and only out-of-state buck in 1982 while hunting the Smoky Mountains in Tennessee. He also learned that the group, Alabama, came out with their signature song, *Mountain Music,* during that same year.

In 1999, Montgomery Gentry released their hit, *Daddy Won't Sell the Farm*. That same year, Amos's neighbors sold out and now a Wal-Mart borders his small farm. But Amos would not sell. When the bulldozers arrived on the neighboring land, a large bodied 10-pointer moved onto Amos's place. Amos shot this great buck on Thanksgiving morning of that year.

Trent concluded his interview with a notion that he had been kicking around in his head. Trent asked Amos if he would like to hunt on his dad's farm this upcoming season. Amos rubbed his beard and slowly nodded his head "yes" then responded, "I would love to see some *new country*."

The following Saturday, Amos showed up at the farm to scout. The farm had thick fence rows, food plots, water and plenty of cover. At the end of the day, Amos asked Trent if he could hunt a small farrow field up by the road, "so as not to interfere with you and your dad's spots," he added. Trent and his dad had blinds overlooking the food plots. They had not really spent much time near the road, but he allowed the legendary deer hunter to do as he wished.

Twenty minutes after first light, a loud shot is heard ringing across the land from the location that Amos chose to hunt. Trent drives his dad over to the farrow field where they see Amos standing over the biggest buck ever killed on their land. This buck has it all; mass, height and width. The men congratulate Amos on his success and the veteran hunter humbly thanks them for the invite. The men load the big buck into the back of Trent's truck as the radio is finishing up a Luke Bryan tune and immediately lights into a Jason Aldean song, *Dirt Road Anthem*. Amos keeps to the beat by tapping his knee to the rhythm of the hard-driving country tunes. Trent looks at the legend and asks, "What are you thinking?"

Amos smiles and replies, "I heard this song the day that we scouted your place, I like this *new country* in more ways than one!"

Bucket List

Sitting quietly in the dark waiting for the wakening of morning gives oneself ample time to think. As two raccoons noisily fight in the swamp, my mind ponders the term, *bucket list*; a list of things to do before you, "kick the bucket."

Where would I start? Personally, I feel that I have accomplished quite a list before I ever heard of the pop culture term. Being married to the women of my dreams, two great kids, a nice house with garage and multiple bathrooms, new truck, great church family, school board member and president of the local National Wild Turkey Federation chapter, what else is there?

Truth be told, *bucket list* practitioners are usually referencing adventurous activities. We all have our dreams and if given the opportunity, my dream list would be filled with wild hunting adventures.

Competing for the top of the list would be a trip to Alaska stalking massive bull-moose with archery tackle. Punching an arrow through the tough hide of a huge bull as his ultra-wide antlers reflect the northern sun would truly be a dream come true. I would then want to glass the valleys for a monster grizzly and successfully stalk to within rifle range and place a lethal bullet into the king of the forest. I picture my trembling hands lifting the powerful paws of the massive bruin and think of the possible dangers that this awesome animal could inflict on moose or man.

Some dreams are hard for me to imagine, such as big horn ram or mountain goat hunting. Physically tackling the mountains as my years start to accumulate and the finances that go along with such an endeavor seem hard to comprehend. The sheer excitement of accomplishing such a feat on either scale would be very rewarding; I picture the view from the top of the mountain as I pose with these two coveted trophies.

My mind suddenly heads south and I find myself standing next to a tall pine as a bugling bull elk approaches through the timber. I then picture myself punching an arrow into his tawny hide and listening as the big bull goes on a death run before noisily crashing to the forest floor. The thin mountain air is surprisingly refreshing as I try to regain my composure. Seeing the long, tall antlers rising up from behind a downed tree is an amazing sight to behold. I no sooner grab an antler when my mind shifts gears and I am traveling in the back of a safari vehicle in pursuit of African cape buffalo.

The Dark Continent's blazing sun heats up as I stalk to within fifty yards of a massive dagga bull. My shot hits true, but fear runs through my entire being as we track the injured bull into thick cover. My heart feels like it is in my throat and relief sweeps through my sweating, adrenaline-pumped body when the PH calls out that he is down for the count. As I kneel beside the dead bull, I feel someone tapping me on the leg.

The tapping continues until I awaken and my son whispers, "Dad, wake up. I think the turkeys are going to fly down."

It is clearly no longer dark and morning has arrived. Three toms land in the green field and commence to gobbling. My son nervously gets his gun into position as I softly work a slate call. The toms hammer out simultaneous gobbles and start walking toward our hen and jake decoys. One minute later, the shotgun barks and the bigger of the two birds hits the turf. My son flashes one of the most beautiful smiles in the whole wide world, and I return with an equally big grin.

When we get home with our desired prize, my heart feels like it is going to burst through my chest as my wife and daughter greet us with huge welcoming smiles and my son blurts out his story in excitable bursts. At this moment, reality trumps any distant event and I am *living* my bucket list. Thank you, Lord, for all that I have been gifted!

Campfire Stories
(Real Life Adventures)

Amazing Africa: Tusk, Thorns & Horns!

While working in Kalamazoo, Michigan, I met an avid hunter named David Wilkins. Yes, there really is a Kalamazoo! The city was the original home of Gibson Guitars and Shakespeare Fishing Tackle. Both of these fine items have provided many happy experiences in hunting camps around the world. Dave had just returned from a plains-game bowhunting safari with his good friend, Gene Wensel. Now I was well aware of Mr. Wensel. The traditional bowhunter was widely known in the *whitetail community* for taking big Montana bucks and for his popular books, *Hunting Rutting Whitetails* and *One Man's Whitetail*.

Dave told me that he planned on returning to the Dark Continent and that I ought to go with him. Oh sure, I had read many adventurous tales about African hunting, but I didn't think that there would ever be a realistic or fiscal chance for me to take such a journey. My personal dream destinations were more along the line of Colorado elk, Alaskan moose and monster bucks in Illinois or Iowa.

I thanked Dave for the offer but respectfully declined. Well, Dave didn't take "no" as an answer; and a few years later I was on a plane that arrived in Johannesburg twenty plus hours after departure.

Our hunting lodge was a three hour drive north of Johannesburg and located about ten miles from the Botswana border. It was pretty cool seeing Kudu crossing signs along the roadside. The South African habitat resembles that of Texas. Short spindly trees and shrubs grow out of sandy soils and like barbwire and roses; literally everything is covered in thorns. Every day I left DNA via sweat and blood in this hostile environment!

Dave and I arrived at our destination shortly after sunset and met our guides / professional hunters (PH) from Sumsare Safaris. Sumsare (pronounced Soom-sar-ee) is the name Erasmus spelled backwards, which was the name of the head PH, Gerard Erasmus. Dave had hunted with Gerard on his previous visit and was eager to meet up with him again. In addition, we met the other PH, Fanie, (pronounced Fawny) who would be paired up with me for the next ten days. We got acquainted around a campfire which became a nightly ritual under the brightly shining stars that make up the Southern Cross. I asked the men about the famous Black Mamba snakes that are rated in every deadliest snake list. They indicated that they had seen some and told me what to do if I got bit; I was to find a shade tree and sit down. The reason was that I might as well enjoy the shade of a tree for the last two minutes of my life rather than bake in the hot sun!

Africa is widely known for its vast variety and high number of available game. In hunter's terms, it is a target-rich environment. Our shopping list of desired trophies included kudu, impala, gemsbok, blesbok, warthog, wildebeest and zebra. Other game available included eland, nylala, hartebeest, bushbuck, duiker, waterbok and baboon. Gerard informed me that I was going to be placed in the baboon hide (blind) the following morning. These Africans view baboons as a nuisance animal, and they instructed me to shoot one if given the chance at no extra charge.

DAY 1

The Greater Kudu is regarded as the most coveted game animal in the world, and it topped our list of most desired trophy. Shortly after sunrise on Day One, Fanie and I went to our designated hide. We bumped a mature kudu off the waterhole that we would be posted at for the day. I had mixed emotions, I was glad to see the game animal on the very first morning that I traveled half way around the world to hunt but disappointed that we scared him off. Fanie and I climbed into a very spacious, elevated, thatched-roof hide and settled in for the day.

Our waterhole sat at the base of a tall rock mountain. Baboons were housed on the mountain and greeted us with raucous barking. Wild, wild Africa, this was going to be fun!

Once our driver left in the truck, the curious baboons made their descent down the mountain to investigate. These creatures are very intelligent and were suspicious of our hut. They held up out of bow range barking and pacing back and forth trying to look into our hideout. Eventually some of the younger animals came in to eat and drink. A big male gorilla continued to hold up in the distance so I targeted him. This beast was vicious. I saw him literally bite the heads of his companions and throw them with a shake of his own head when they got too close to his feed. Gerard's girlfriend shared with us an unpleasant experience that she and her sister had in which they helplessly watched a group of baboons attack and tear apart the family dog, limb by limb.

The gorilla was slowly making his way into bow range as I prepared myself to take the shot. Before I could do so, a herd of thirty or more impala suddenly came to the waterhole. A North American comparison to the African impala would be the whitetail deer. Impalas also have incredible leaping ability and their leaps give off an incredible illusion of freeze-framing suspension in the middle of their thirty-five foot jumps. Extremely numerous, I saw more of this species than any other. One of the last animals in the herd was a large ram. I pointed him out to Fanie and he very matter of factly said, "He is a nice one, you should shoot him." At this point, I totally forgot about the baboon and focused on the trophy ram. From a sitting position, I pulled back my 70-pound Matthews Feather Max bow and placed my pin tight behind the impala's small shoulder. It would be a simple fifteen yard shot, but I had to hold my draw until a smaller ram moved from behind the animal that I wanted to shoot. As soon as the second animal cleared out, I touched the release and watched the ram jump sideways with what looked like a good hit.

I leaped to my feet and looked out another window asking Fanie if the shot was good. Fanie surprised me with an immediate response of, "Yes, he's down, good shot."

Looking further to the right, I saw the ram lying on a large slab of rock forty yards away from the blind. I was one happy hunter! The beautiful impala was a wonderful African trophy and a great boost to my confidence. Spending the rest of the day in the blind, we observed more impala, small warthogs and waterbuck. The baboons could be seen and heard back up on the mountain, but they did not return after my shot disturbed their feeding and watering.

GREATER KUDU

On the second day, we went to a pit blind that had lots of trophy warthog sign. We saw more impala and waterbuck. Numerous warthogs visited the waterhole but the trophy boars failed to appear. Mid-afternoon, I saw my first kudu from a blind. There was a bachelor group of five juveniles. They all presented fifteen to twenty yard shots.

When the bright orange sun descended low onto the horizon, the bright light irritated our eyes. Seeking relief from the glaring sun, I looked to my far right and saw a majestic sight. A large, mature kudu bull was standing broadside thirty yards away. He looked magnificent! His horns twisted and turned high into the sky and carried the much-desired *deep curls*. Although I was confident that I could make the shot, it was early in the hunt, and I gambled that the Greater Kudu would come in closer like the bachelor group did earlier. The gamble paid off.

I had been picturing this very moment for months and now my African dream was standing slightly quartering away at a mere twelve yards. I was at full draw. Everything was as it should be except one thing. We were filming the hunt and Fanie couldn't see the kudu due to the blinding sun. Fanie was filming over my shoulder and kept repeating in my ear, "Don't shoot." We attempted to move a little bit closer when the large bull startled and ran off. Talk about frustrating!

Neither Fanie nor I thought the big bull would return. Just in case he did return though, we devised a way to mount the camera on the ledge of the window. We now had less than an hour of light left.

A half hour later, Fanie looked to our right and saw that my highly desired trophy had actually returned. Fanie pushed the record button and then backed out of the way. Unbelievably, the big bull came right in and presented the exact same shot. I drew, placed my pin low behind the shoulder and let the arrow fly.

The shot looked like a carbon copy of the one I had made a day earlier on the impala. Fanie repeated, "Good shot, my friend. Good shot, my friend."

The kudu splashed across the water, ran fifty yards and stopped. Blood could be seen cresting the opposite shoulder indicating a clean pass through and good shot placement. The bull then slowly walked out of sight into the thick African bush. I was confident that he quickly went down.

Fifteen minutes later our ride arrived and the four of us went in search of my much-desired trophy. Surprisingly, we followed blood for a couple hundred yards and the two PHs decided that we should back out and look in the morning. This was not comforting, especially since we had seen a jackal (North American comparison would be a coyote) at the waterhole earlier in the evening.

The following morning, Dave, Gerard, Fanie and I resumed tracking the injured bull. Unbelievably, we tracked the large antelope for two hours and traveled well over a mile. I was greatly concerned that this amazing animal was going to go unfound, and I was going to have to pay a tremendous trophy fee for an animal that appeared to be lethally hit. About this time, Gerard stopped and quietly brought us together. Gerard pointed to the sandy soil and whispered, "He's tiring, look how his hooves are splaying; we should find him soon."

New hope ran through my veins and a short time later, we jumped the kudu out of his bed. My mind was reeling. I was quite surprised that he was still alive. Gerard took off running and I followed closely behind him. We jogged for about one hundred yards and then walked very quickly for another couple of hundred yards. Occasionally, Gerard would glance at the ground but kept a quick pace. Eventually, he slowed down and then abruptly stopped and stared into the bush. We stood still for a short spell but I didn't see anything. I then asked in a low whisper, "Do you see him?"

Gerard shook his head "no" and whispered back, "No, I hear him hitting his horns in the brush. He is quite sick."

We then quietly advanced forward until we saw the bull standing under a tree shaking his head back and forth with his horns rattling against the branches. A second shot ended the long ordeal.

I was extremely elated to have gotten such a magnificent animal but also baffled that a seemingly *perfect* shot could have such poor results. Later we learned that only one lung was hit. This fine bull proved his toughness and lived up to his name, GREATER KUDU!

Dave and Fanie soon caught up with us and we all admired the sheer beauty of this magnificent animal. We took numerous pictures and measured him at 52 inches. In preparing for my trip to Africa, I had read Fred Bear's book, *Field Notes*. Fred wrote, "It had been beyond my fondest hopes to bag a kudu with the bow and arrow but there it was lying before me, glistening in the sun." What a great memory!

Dave arrowed a kudu the following day and experienced a much shorter tracking experience. Dave's trophy carried a very unique wide spread.

WARTHOGS

Gerard and Fanie both told me that I needed to shoot a warthog while in Africa. They also said that they were very tough animals and no matter where you place an arrow, a warthog would run at least one hundred yards.

Although there are many marvels in this amazing land, it is truly incredible the vast amount of wild game that you see. One of the largest populations is that of the warthogs. A barrel-chested tusker was definitely on my wish list.

By the third day of the hunt, I had seen hundreds of warthogs but no trophy boars. Gerard told me to shoot the first boar to come that morning because he needed bait for a leopard hunter. Early in the morning, a juvenile boar came in all by himself. Once again, I was hunting from an elevated shooting house. The warthog was standing broadside twenty five yards away. When I shot, I watched the arrow hit low. The hog took a side-step further out and I saw the arrow lying flat on the ground.

Did I miss? This question flashed through my mind for a brief second as the hog stood in place.

What happened next confirmed a lethal hit. The mad tusker started spinning in a circle like the Warner Brothers cartoon character, The Tasmanian Devil. A dust cloud developed and hung in the air. The hog came out of his spin, made a mad dash for about fifty yards then started spinning again. He then ran a straight line back towards us before tipping over about twenty yards away.

The arrow had passed directly through the heart. Excitement filled the hunting hut and when we settled down, we decided to rewind the video camera and watch the show again. As fate would have it, Fanie failed to hit the record button so we didn't preserve the magical moment on film after all.

Even though I saw several warthogs, I had yet to lay my eyes on a big trophy boar. Dave was seeing shooters at one particular waterhole and encouraged me to hunt there. Sitting in a brushed in, double-bull ground blind, I soon had over twenty hogs feeding within thirty yards of my hide. Once again, they were all females or juvenile males. An hour later, I finally saw what I was looking for. Out of a thicket stepped the Grand Pumbaa. Instead of running over to feed like the rest of his hombres, he stood off in the distance surveying the scene. It was as if he, rather than Simba, was the King of the Land.

For forty-five minutes, Your Highness stood off in the distance stretching, rubbing his back and tusks on trees, and in general, strutting his stuff. When he finally came within bow range, I drew my bow and attempted to hold the pin on his shoulder. This proved to be a difficult task because of his constant shifting and the other hogs getting in the way. After a lengthy stretch of time, I had to let down on my draw. When I was within a mere inch of accomplishing this, I inadvertently touched the release and my arrow had just enough energy to slice through the camouflaged mesh window and stick in the mud; a meager three feet from the blind.

Naturally, this disturbance caused the whole herd of pigs to scatter towards the cover. The trophy boar that I wanted to shoot stopped at the edge of the cover and defiantly stared back. While the rest of the herd watched, Grand Pumbaa puffed out his mighty chest and unbelievably marched right back to the exact same spot. What had taken forty minutes to do earlier, now took less than two minutes. The prideful pig stood solely in place and presented an easy shot. This time I drew and shot, burying the arrow deep into his shoulder.

The heart shot hog made a mad dash into an extra-large stump, crashed to the ground, jumped high into the air and then fell flat out dead fifty yards away. This time the whole sequence was successfully caught on film. The Thunderhead fixed blade broadhead worked wonderfully on the thick-hided brute. Gerard and Fanie were right. Warthogs provided some great bowhunting action!

BLESBOK

Some would say that blesbok resemble goats. They are the color of chocolate and possess a white face. Both the male and female blesbok have ribbed horns similar in shape to the springbok which is the national animal of South Africa but not found in our area.

Like most of the plain's game, these animals run with a herd. If you see one, then probably six to ten others are nearby. One herd of seven kept walking by a particular hide but would not commit until my second to last day of hunting. This particular herd only had one male so there was only one possible target. As fate would have it, the blesbok came to the waterhole, and the male was the closest and only one who presented a shot. I drew my bow but had to wait for the other blesbok to move. Otherwise, there was a good chance that one of them would be shot if the arrow passed through the male.

Fortunately for me, the females pulled out one by one and the male was the last one left to drink. I had held my draw for almost two full minutes and when I shot, my arrow hit farther back than I wanted. All week long Fanie had praised me with the same compliment, "Good shot, my friend." However, with this shot, his comments were quite different. When the arrow hit, Fanie barked out, "Bad shot, you gut shot him. Get another arrow quick, you gut shot him, bad shot!"

Ouch! As I scrambled to knock a second arrow, the injured blesbok ran into the thorny barriers placed along the outer banks of the waterhole. It took three or four attempts to find his way out but when he did, he was gone without me getting in a second shot. Fanie continued to mutter, "Bad shot," as if I needed to be reminded!

During my two week safari, I found the South African people to be very blunt. They didn't mince words and spoke their mind. I was ok with that. I appreciate people who are straight shooters.

Well, luck was on my side and the blesbok only ran fifty yards before toppling over dead. My arrow had actually exited behind the opposite shoulder and sliced through both lungs. I admit that I failed to hit where I was shooting but was very happy with the desired outcome. In this case, it was better to be lucky than good; whereas in the previous hunt with the Kudu, I placed the arrow where I wanted but had a drastically different outcome!

ZEBRA

High on my wish list was zebra. Their gorgeous skins make for a great rug. I have seen where some people have upholstered furniture with this fine leather. Unfortunately, the zebras proved to be most elusive and would not come to the waterholes during the daylight hours. We would occasionally see them in the area but they would never come within archery range.

We were the last group of hunters for the year. Even though we were on a bowhunting safari, I asked Gerard if we could try to get a zebra with a gun since they were only drinking at night. Gerard approved of this, so the following day we went in search of the striped horses. We went to a waterhole where the zebras had been seen on the perimeters and found lots of tracks. The next move surprised me. There was one lone tall tree and Gerard climbed it to scan the surrounding landscape. Gerard climbed to the very top and perched himself a good fifty to sixty feet off the ground. This crazy maneuver intrigued me so I took pictures. Gerard turned around and stated in a slightly agitated tone, "What are you doing? Taking pictures so that you can show people the crazy African?"

I shrugged and replied matter of factly, "Yeah!"

Although Gerard climbed the tree, he did not find the zebras so two trackers were given a radio and told to follow the tracks into the bush. Just before noon, a small herd of seven were found. I first spotted them several hundred yards out in some rare open land with scattered brush. One of the seven was a stallion. Half way into our stalk, we spooked a small herd of previously unseen kudu, which in turn spooked the zebras. For the next hour, we were able to trail them from the truck. Gerard, Dave and I rode in the back while Fanie drove. The kudu spotted us on our second stalk as well and after this, they herded up with the zebra.

We now wanted to separate the kudu from the zebras and Fanie successfully accomplished this by driving the truck toward the herd. The kudu went one way and the zebra the other.

Much later into the day, we finally stalked to within one hundred yards of the zebra and the stallion was identified. I found the zebra in the crosshairs of the scoped 7 mm rifle and pulled the trigger. The stallion jumped and then ran off with the rest of the herd. Gerard looked at me and dryly asked, "Did you miss?"

I replied, "I don't think so. I thought he jumped like he was hit."

We walked to where the zebra had stood and found no blood or hair. Trailing their tracks provided no sign of a hit either. At this point, we decided to look at the video footage that Dave had taken. When we watched the tape, we saw a small tree throw debris. Further investigation revealed that the bullet hit a small tree and had deflected the bullet. I was just thankful that I didn't wound this wonderful creature. How ironic, I was near perfect with archery gear only missing a baboon at forty-five yards and yet I missed with a gun at an easy distance.

As we drove back to the lodge that last night, we took in an amazing site. We were traveling along a rock outcropping when we saw a large kudu standing on a small shelf looking over his royal kingdom. He looked like a monument placed there to remind us of the grandeur that makes up Africa. We parked the truck and simply took in this awesome sight. He stood completely still for at least a full minute. Eventually, the magnificent monarch turned and scrambled up and over what looked like a vertical rock with the apparent ease of a Rocky Mountain Ram. What a wonderful and grand farewell!

AMAZING AFRICA

All in all, I was thankful for the opportunity of stalking wild game on this amazing continent. Hunting African game did not replace my love for North American game but instead, it enhanced my appreciation for all things wild. The new experiences were exhilarating. I experienced totally new sights, smells and sounds. God's creation is wonderfully big and diverse. Someday, I hope to return and hunt gemsbok, wildebeest, cape buffalo and zebra. However, even if I never make it back, I captured amazing memories that have invigorated my soul and will last a lifetime. If you ever get the chance for yourself, I have one word of advice "GO!"

Glorious Mornings

Look up *Glorious Mornings* in a dictionary and I think that you should be able to see a photograph of a spring sunrise in turkey habitat. After a long cold winter, spring is a welcome sight. In 2011, my first hunt during Michigan's May season was simply spectacular. God's glory radiated and invigorated my soul.

I set up in the dark under a ceiling of sparkling stars. My gear consisted of an Ameri-Step Doghouse pop-up blind, a camouflage bag chair, two decoys (jake & hen) and a camouflage Mossberg 12-gauge, loaded with Winchester 5 shot. Of course, I was also wearing a turkey vest filled with various calls. I sat on the southern edge of a recently plowed field. The field's northern border had a row of trees that housed roosting birds.

An owl hooted and a boss tom gobbled a powerful

response. What a wonderful sound! A few more gobbles boomed in the darkness before the stars faded completely away. When light arrived, I saw the trophy tom standing proudly in his tree, all puffed out in full strut. Soon thereafter, the tom flew down and disappeared into a low spot in the field. Four other previously, unseen birds flew down and joined him. I struck out some quiet purrs and yelps on my slate call and patiently waited. Two hen heads were the first to crest the hill in front of me. They ate their way across the field and passed by at forty-five yards. Song birds continuously flitted around and serenaded me throughout the hunt. Two other hens appeared to my left and they had the big tom following them while he remained in full strut. The warm sun rose, which illuminated the landscape and reflected brilliantly off of the tom's effervescent feathers. His head was a bright bluish-white spectacle. My pleading calls were ignored, and I watched the trio s-l-o-w-l-y walk away for the next hour and a half with no chance for a stalk.

The next morning, I returned to the exact same spot. Tommy was once again gobbling on the roost and flew with his harem down into the low spot. On this day, five heads popped up over the hill, and they were advancing straight for me. Four hens and a jake marched in formation with the Boss Gobbler following the procession about twenty to thirty yards behind them. The front row of birds closed the distance quickly and I ranged them for fifty yards. My adrenaline kicked into overdrive when the totally unexpected happened. The tom had seemed to notice the decoys for the first time and started retreating all the while gobbling a command for the hens to join him. The girls abruptly stopped and actually turned around and casually followed Mr. Bossy Pants away from me. The jake stood all alone in the field and looked totally perplexed. The juvenile male then saw the decoys as an opportunity and came walking in. Jacob was within five yards of me but the 12-gauge remained quiet because at this point I wanted his older friend, the cagey tom whom I had already nicknamed *my nemesis.*

When the field was empty, I packed up so that I could make it to my daughter's soccer game. As I walked out, I couldn't help but think that my wife, Michelle, would have loved the sights and sounds that my morning hunt had offered. She does not want to shoot anything herself, but she has been very supportive of me. I have encouraged her to at least experience a hunt and she has indicated that she would do so. I have told her that I thought turkey season would be ideal because there is always an abundance of game and the weather is usually quite mild. There was no doubt in my mind that Michelle would appreciate a *glorious morning* in turkey country, and I was anxious to share the fun.

The following Saturday morning, Michelle had the grand opportunity of waking up at 4:15 a.m. I noticed that it had rained a little in the night and had actually warmed up quite a bit as well. When we arrived at the farm, everything was soaking wet. As I unloaded the truck, I immediately noticed something else different from the previous *glorious mornings.* Mosquitoes swarmed the truck. Fortunately, I had packed that wonderful bug repelling invention called a

Thermacell, and I would fire it up as soon as we got to our set-up.

Getting to our stand location proved to be a daunting task. Personally, I had no problem navigating the edge of the plowed field, but apparently Michelle thought that it would have been a good idea if I had brought along a flashlight. Flipping my cell phone open repeatedly to provide light didn't seem to help when my 6 foot 1 inch gate would distance me from her 5 foot 2 inch strides. As it turned out, walking a muddy plowed field in the dark was not exactly her idea of fun.

When we finally made it to the stand site, the mosquitoes once again swarmed around us. We both put our hoods up until I assembled our gear (tent, chairs, decoys). Once we were finally settled into our chairs, I hurriedly got the Thermacell out. As luck would have it, the apparatus would choose this morning for the igniter to fail. Repeated attempts did not succeed and I deemed the now worthless tool, officially broken! Michelle coped by placing her elbows on her knees and covering her face with her hands while pressing her hood tight against her ears. Fortunately for me, the trophy tom was once again roosted over the swamp and he let out a couple of gobbles. When I excitedly asked Michelle if she heard him, she nodded her head in a matter to indicate that it wasn't as joyous a sound for her as it was for me. It probably would have sounded better without the humming from the squadron of mosquitoes buzzing the air!

When daylight arrived, the mosquitoes actually dispersed, and Michelle was able to set up her brand new camera so that she could film this memorable occasion. The big tom flew to a bare limb making him easy to see. Michelle caught a glimpse and attempted to zoom in on him. While trying to get the turkey into focus, the big bird flew down into the low spot. No other birds joined him on this day's fly-down so I thought that he would run right over to my sweet talking hen talk. Michelle didn't record the bird in the tree but she would soon be able to once the turkey climbed over the hill. The gobbler responded with loud gobbles and did so consistently for the next half-hour as he walked AWAY from us OUT-OF-SIGHT! All Michelle saw of the majestic bird was the brief glimpse in the tree.

With the Trophy Tom out of hearing range, my ears heard a gentle tapping on the roof of the blind indicating that it had started to rain lightly. Being the expert that I am on all things turkey, I whispered to Michelle that this could be a good thing because turkeys seek out open fields during a rain. Needless-to-say, Michelle did not see this as a *good thing* when the lightly tapping rain turned into a tropical downpour and the powerful H2O swiftly filtered through the thin tent roof. To say the least, we quickly packed our gear and I led my rain-soaked bride back across the now sloppy, mud-bog called a field. No flashlight was needed but an umbrella would have been good!

As we walked through the mud, my mind kept racing with the same thought, "What was I thinking? I don't even hunt turkeys in a hard rain and here I go taking my wife out on her inaugural hunt in a downpour." Lucky for me, I chose a farm close to home so I was able to get Michelle into our dry house, which of course had a good supply of dry clothes.

My intentions were good that May morning and Michelle actually rolled with it quite well. Hunting is not always about getting your prey; rather it is about the memories and the stories that come with it. In that regard, I provided Michelle with a true hunting adventure. Like all of us who hunt, she has a great story to share about the time her hunt-crazy husband took her out in the dark without a flashlight to *enjoy* a mosquito-ridden journey through a muddy field to sit in a tropical downpour all for the purpose of killing a turkey which went the other way! She has had good-spirited fun sharing this tale with me serving the role of the protagonist. Michelle's dictionary would probably describe a *glorious morning* a bit different than mine. Her dictionary would have a picture of a fireplace, a warm cup of Chi and the sun filtering through the window of the cabin as it rises over a lake. Will Michelle return to the turkey woods? I think so but I know that when that time comes, she will be packing a flashlight, a working Thermacell and a forecast of sunshine! I can hardly wait!

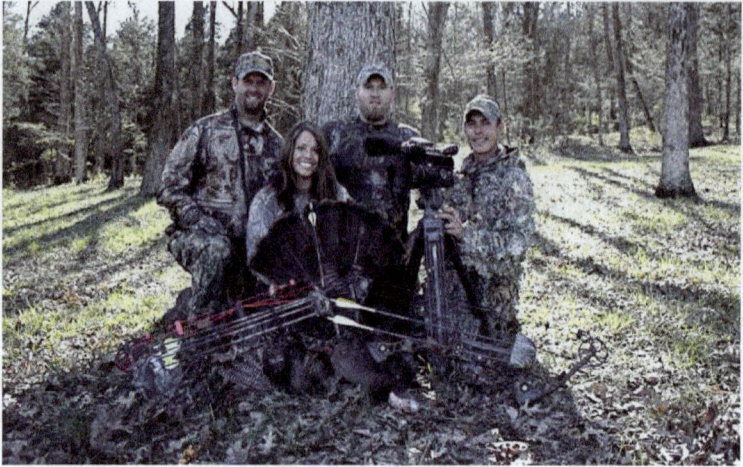

Tag Team

Glen Roberts is a man of action. Glen works for a company that sets up the red carpet events in Nashville, Tennessee, and prepares the various venues so that the country music stars can shine. During his off time, Glen pursues his two passions in life; dirt biking and hunting. He is the everyday working man version of country music singer, Craig Morgan, who also enjoys these same two hobbies. According to Glen, "I would rather quit breathing before I quit hunting."

To no one's surprise, Glen married a gal named Marla who is equally passionate about hunting. While the number of hunters dwindles with each passing year, the one demographic that continues to grow is women hunters. The outdoor television industry reflects this trend with many programs highlighting married couples pursuing wild game. Glen and Marla have a log cabin home in the hills of

Tennessee and chase after a variety of critters literally in their own backyard.

On the opening day of the Tennessee firearm deer season in 2007, Glen elected to ride his dirt bike across the road from his home with some friends before partaking in the evening hunt. Glen hit a jump that he had done a thousand times before but on this fateful day something went wrong. According to Glen, "When I went off the jump, the front of the bike dove down and I thought it was going to flip over and land on me. So, I bailed. Instead of sliding like I planned, my feet stuck to the tacky clay and slung me forward. I did a textbook *scorpion* (scorpion – a particularly nasty fall where a rider lands on their face/chest, causing their back to arch and their legs to bend over their head as they slide across the ground). While my face was planted in the dirt, the rest of my body flipped over my head!"

Emergency personnel came quickly to the scene of the crash and a helicopter flew Glen to the hospital. Marla was obviously quite distraught and kept remembering something that Glen had told her on more than one occasion. Glen had told her that he was going to die at the age of 30 in a motorcycle accident. Glen was now 30 years of age and barely hanging on to his life.

Marla describes herself as a spiritual person and states that she continued to pray throughout the ordeal. When she finally left the hospital to go home, she prayed for God to give her a sign that Glen would be all right. When she pulled into her driveway, a big white owl landed right in front of her causing her to have to stop the vehicle. At that point, Marla knew that this was her sign, and she had faith that Glen would pull through.

Glen had shattered his C-2 vertebra and fractured his C-3 vertebra. He was completely paralyzed for a few days and his right side remained paralyzed for an additional couple of weeks. Glen told me, "I have what they call *Browns-Sequard Syndrome*. I have loss of motor skill functions on my right side and loss of sensation on my left, not to mention some new *bling* inside my neck. I've got two rods and ten screws extending from my C-4 vertebra to the base of my skull. "

Glen's rehab was intense. He literally had to learn how to do everything again. He couldn't walk, go to the bathroom, or even feed himself. Glen states that the physical recovery was nothing compared to the emotional and mental recovery. Glen goes on to say, "I was an extremely active person and going from wide open to a totally dependent state was almost too much to bear. I kept telling myself that I wanted to be able to go hunting again. During the second week of my hospitalization, I was lying in bed with my mother standing on one side and my wife on the other. At this point, there had been no movement in my right side and I was pretty discouraged. Then I tried, like so many times before, to move my hand. I just stared at it and screamed while giving it all I had, then my index finger (or trigger finger as I call it) twitched. There was not a dry eye on that hospital floor. From that day on, it was game on! Two weeks later, I walked out of there!!!"

Once Glen got home, he continued to work diligently on his rehabilitation. He was determined to go bowhunting and tried to pull back Marla's bow but failed. Through intensive work, Glen is once again able to pull back his 70-pound bow. Due to the fact that he can't turn his head, Glen shoots right handed but uses his left eye to aim. The professionals at Bay Archery customized his sights to stick WAY out to the left. Glen laughs, "It looks goofy but it works. It's a lot like me!"

Through their Nashville connections, the married couple became friends with Daniel White, who is the brother of country music singer, Bryan White. Glen took Daniel out for his first bowhunting adventure and eventually Daniel shot his first whitetail, a 6-point buck. From that point on, Daniel was hooked on bowhunting and even got his brother, Bryan, hooked as well.

Bryan lined up an archery turkey hunt with the Roger Raglin Outdoor Television Show and brought Daniel, Glen and Marla on the hunt as well. Roger and the White brothers missed a few turkeys so the crew did not have any successful kills filmed. Towards the end of the week, a cameraman went out with Marla along with another man who called and used the technique called *fanning*. With this procedure, a person gets low to the ground and decoys a tom into shooting range by displaying a turkey fan. On this particular day, the maneuver worked wonderfully and a big tom was moving towards Marla's location.

Unbeknownst to Marla was the fact that her husband had chosen to use an old barn as a blind. Marla and her two companions were calling/decoying the bird in a manner that would provide Glen with a shot opportunity before the tom would get to them. Glen saw the turkey, pulled back his 70-pound bow and released an arrow that passed through the trophy tom. The bird jumped up and did a 360 degree flip. When the bird landed back on its feet, Marla had no idea that the bird was shot and took her own shot. Marla was thirty yards out but her arrow also hit home. Neither Glen nor Marla had previously shot a turkey with archery tackle and now the husband and wife team had successfully tag-teamed on a trophy tom. How cool is that? Marla's cameraman captured the memorable moment on film, and the hunt appeared on Roger's Television Show in the fall of 2011.

The mature tom had a beard measuring ten and a half inches and sported one inch spurs. The Roberts got a full body-mount, which proudly testifies, to the tag teaming efforts of this married hunting twosome.

To say that Glen's accident has been life changing would be an understatement in the physical sense but in the mental game, it reinforces Glen's attitude toward living a full life. "Live life fully because you never know what tomorrow may offer."

Through God's grace, Glen and Marla continue in their tag team quest for big game and often open up their home and property to share the great outdoors with others. Glen states that what he likes most these days is helping others get started out in hunting. "There is nothing more rewarding to me than helping someone else achieve success in the outdoors. Watching someone shaking out of control after shooting their first deer is just awesome. It is something that truly cannot be explained but must be experienced."

Glen adds that while Marla received the gift of the white owl as a sign from God that everything was going to be alright, he has received a similar sign from an albino deer. The white deer has periodically appeared on the hill across the road from his home, exactly where the jump is located.

Glen and Marla both aspire to harvest Rocky Mountain elk. I'm betting that it will be a tag team effort. Happy hunting Mr. and Mrs. Roberts; your story has inspired many!

Go Green!

Go Green! Everywhere I turn someone is telling me to *Go Green*. A former American Vice President travels the country in a private jet and lectures the public on saving energy. Hollywood celebrities armed with their highly knowledgeable theater degrees administer energy-saving advice before retreating back to their energy-guzzling mansions.

Personally, I thought that I went green almost three

decades ago when I attended Michigan State University. I even stood in the stands at the football games and shouted out with the rest of the student body; *Go Green*!

Now I am told that there is a Green Movement and that their purpose is to create an environmentally friendly world. Once again, I am glad to announce that I was way out in front of the curve. In the 1990s, I purchased recreational property and planted vibrant green pine and spruce trees. These trees, as opposed to jets, mansions, pavement etc., aid in replenishing oxygen to our environment and offer security cover to native wildlife.

As an American citizen, I am also barraged with requests from famous individuals much richer than myself, to give financially to their chosen environmental cause. These causes may or may not be giving the money to aiding our environment. Fortunately, I don't have to listen to their opinions of where I spend my money because I already donate money to environmental causes. I am a proud member of the largest fraternity of conservationists in the world. I am a hunter and we hunters donate more time and money to protecting wildlife and wildlife habitat than any other group on the planet. According to Wikipedia, in 1937, hunters successfully lobbied Congress to pass the Pittman-Robertson Wildlife Restoration Act, which placed 11% tax on all hunting equipment. This self-imposed tax now generates $700 million each year and is used exclusively to establish, restore and protect wildlife habitat.

Many hunters, including myself, also contribute extra funds to special interest groups. One of these groups, The National Wild Turkey Federation, in concert with the

Michigan Department of Resources, has helped me and other hunters across southern Michigan to *Go Green* every spring. Starting in the 1980s, these two groups re-introduced turkeys to this region of Michigan; and their efforts have led to a thriving turkey population that I and others, now have the opportunity to hunt every spring. Partaking in this annual activity is now my favorite method of *Going Green*. My eyes feast on the green landscape after a long winter of visual black and white. Every day afield in late April and early May is absolutely magical in its transforming of new growth. You can literally hunt a new environment daily even while hunting the same parcel of land. You can start out before first light in freezing temperatures and return later in the afternoon to 70 degree sunshine.

On a mid-May afternoon, I sneaked through some of those pines that I had planted years earlier and sat amongst them while glassing a field that had recently been plowed. After sitting awhile, I spotted a lone tom along the opposite field edge. I then stalked to a closer location and positioned myself next to an ancient oak tree that may remember from its youth, the original turkeys that used to inhabit the land. I then proceeded to hen call at the lonely fellow. He wouldn't even look my way, so I eventually decided to use my gobble call and the challenge worked. He turned in my direction and I began to hammer him with a variety of aggressive hen calls alternating between a box and slate call. When the long-bearded bird got closer, I switched to a push-button call and continued to lure him towards my direction as I lay in ambush under the shade of the freshly clothed oak tree.

When he reached forty yards, his body language indicated that he was about to bolt so I aimed my fully camouflaged 12-gauge at the base of his peri-scoping red neck and pulled the trigger, which promptly anchored the big bird to the plowed turf.

Another wonderful spring turkey season had concluded with the smell of gun powder in the air. Success was mine through the scout, glass, spot and stalk, call, shotgun-go-boom method. Once again, I admired what I call the world's prettiest, ugly bird. The color that radiates off its sheen of feathers is astonishingly beautiful while his shriveled head reminds me of prehistoric creatures. I then chose to scan the surrounding landscape and take it all in. Green growth was abundantly displayed as far as the eye could see. Just like my Michigan State days – my mind shouted, *Go Green*!

Photo Courtesy of Tony Snyder

To Whom Much is Given

I drive up to the guard shack at the Fort Custer Training Center and identify myself to the security guard. He asks for my driver's license and soon thereafter, I am cleared to enter the high-fenced military compound. The guard gives me directions and I slowly drive away. After the first set of buildings, I turn left and drive by an impressive

96

assortment of military vehicles. Next, I slowly drive by a series of gun ranges that are all occupied by camouflaged-attired soldiers shooting assault weapons. At the end of the road, I turn right and enter a wooded area where I see a pavilion and four-wheel drive trucks. I have arrived.

The previous paragraph could explain many places around the world where American soldiers are actively training while heeding the call to serve and protect. This particular base is located in southern Michigan and occupies land in both Kalamazoo and Calhoun Counties. For the past several years, the base has also hosted a Youth Turkey Hunt that they coordinate through the local National Wild Turkey Federation chapter called the Turkeyville Toms.

The 2012 hunt took place on April 27, 28 and 29. Nineteen hunters took advantage of this golden opportunity including a group of three boy scouts who traveled four hours from Traverse City, Michigan. One of the three was a fifteen year old named, Zach, who was teamed up with me. I had the good fortune of serving as Zach's mentor/guide/caller.

I met with Zach at the Friday evening orientation. Sam Giese, president of the Turkeyville Toms, addressed our group, gave us the weekend itinerary and explained the rules. While everyone enjoyed a hot dog dinner, Rick Grosteffon, a two-time Michigan State Champion Turkey Caller demonstrated a variety of calls and explained the basics of turkey hunting.

The orientation was followed by a *turkey shoot* on one of the previously mentioned ranges. Paper targets were set up twenty yards out. Fort Custer staffer, Jonathan

Edgerly, facilitated the shoot to ensure overall safety and proper weapon handling. I sat with Zach and assisted him, as did all of the other mentors with their protégé. Zach had brought a Sears and Roebuck 12-gauge that had belonged to his late grandfather. This young man had never operated the weapon. I showed Zach how to work the safety, load the gun, work the gun's pump action and aim. It was a pure joy to be able to assist this eager beginner. A sense of accomplishment and confidence was apparent when the group of young shooters examined their targets and observed their successful *kills*.

The evening concluded with Zach and I exploring our assigned hunting area. We scouted the rolling hardwood ridges and found *sign* in the form of turkey scratchings on the forest floor. I asked Zach why he chose to come on this hunt. He answered, "I used to enjoy hunting and spending time in the woods with my grandfather. Unfortunately, grandpa died seven years ago of a heart attack while afield on the opening day of the firearm deer season. " The call of the wild was heard much earlier and is still in this young man's heart.

Early Saturday morning, we gathered at 4 a.m. for breakfast and a quick debriefing by Mr. Giese. Mentor, Rick LaFrinere, courteously gifted every youth hunter with a handmade paddle box call. Appreciative smiles lit up the room as the young hunters received their kind gift.

At 5 a.m., we headed out. Cloud cover had moved in during the night and the weather forecast was calling for rain. When we got to our hunt location, Zack grabbed his gun and I carried in a pop-up tent blind and two chairs. Zach and I set up in the dark and I placed a hen and jake decoy set fifteen yards out. Right before first light, I blew into an owl call in an effort to get a roosted tom to gobble a response and give away his location. Throughout the morning, I called utilizing a striker/slate call, a paddle box call and a push button box call. Zach attempted a few calls but we could not get a bird to respond. We shared some Milky Way and Reese candy bars and hunted two different sets.

The rain started falling around 9:30 a.m. At 11 a.m., we decided to head in for lunch and dry out. While driving back, we came upon another team leaving the woods. They were hunting about a half mile north of us in the same section. They had heard a single gobble north of where they were hunting but hadn't seen anything.

When we returned to camp, we discovered that others had a much more productive morning. Five turkeys had been tagged. Four of the birds were killed by first-time hunters. One of Zach's Traverse City friends, Evan, had shot one of the big toms. Evan told us, "We sat in a blind for four hours and nothing happened. We then received a call from another guide whose hunter had already gotten a turkey. He told us that he saw a bird in a different part of our section. So we went over to where the bird was and set up. The guide started calling and the bird came to the call and I got him!"

The *culture* of turkey hunting was truly prevalent. Tony Snyder, the state chapter NWTF president, called in a bird for a young boy named Noah who successfully anchored the tom to the turf. During lunch, Tony shared pictures from his recent trip to South America where he and his wife collected Ocellated turkeys to complete their quest for the Turkey World Slam. A Turkey Grand Slam is accomplished when you kill each of the four United States subspecies (Eastern's, Merriam's, Osceola's and Rio Grand's). When you add a Gould's you achieve a Royal Slam and adding a Ocellated turkey completes the World Slam.

Rick Grosteffon guided a hunter named Josh for the fifth year in a row. Josh accomplished a much desired dream of shooting a turkey with his bow. Rick captured the hunt on his phone and shared the footage to the adorning novice hunters and veteran guides. While we watched, Rick narrated, "We did not hear any gobbling from the roost. I called frequently until a single gobble rang out from behind us. A tom made his way into the decoys, walking within arm's reach of the blind. When Josh drew, he had a huge smile spreading from ear to ear. The shot was perfect and the bird went down within five yards. I don't think that Josh has quit smiling!"

As fate would have it, Zach's crew lit out after lunch on Saturday, so we didn't get to go back out. However, Zach did leave with an outdoor education, a box call and a smile on his face. Two more turkeys were tagged Sunday morning including a double-bearded trophy. Overall, seven of the nineteen hunters shot turkeys in the two-day hunt. Many others experienced close calls with gobbling toms that just wouldn't close the distance. New hunters were born and expertly trained that weekend.

The aforementioned team of Rick and Josh completed their fifth year together of participating in the

Fort Custer Youth Hunt. This was Josh's fourth turkey in five years. When Rick returned the ever-smiling Josh back to his mom, she pulled Rick aside and asserted, "You have no idea what an impact you have had on Josh. Thank You!"

Rick has spent the past few years "paying it forward" by mentoring Josh. Josh will be too old to participate as a hunter next year but has already volunteered to return so that he can give back to the program from which he has greatly received. How cool is that?

The Bible says, "From everyone who has been given much, much will be demanded." Most hunters live the lives that they live because someone took the time to mentor them. What a great way of touching lives in a manner that could be life changing!

Photo Courtesy of Tony Snyder

Hunting with the Judge

The king of hearts sat in my hand when the emcee of the Calhoun County Whitetails Unlimited banquet called out the winning card for a choice of guns spread out on a table, "The Queen of Hearts." Oh so close. Standing next to me was my brother, Jeff, and he was holding the royal lady in red. Jeff did not hesitate with his choice; he pointed at a Taurus Judge revolver and said, "I'll take that one."

The Taurus Judge is a handgun chambered for .410 bore shot shells and the .45 Colt cartridges. The handgun is marketed as a tool for self-defense and home protection but can be successfully used for hunting when a person is disciplined enough to hunt within its restricted range.

Jeff is an avid hunter and his thoughts quickly ventured to, "what can I hunt with this new weapon?" A search of the Michigan Spring Turkey rules found the following; "Hunters may use a bow and arrow, crossbow, *a firearm that fires a fixed shotgun shell* or a muzzleloading shotgun for turkey hunting."

When the 2010 season arrived, Jeff packed his new revolver along with his Bowtech bow, pop-up tent blind, turkey calls and decoys. The veteran turkey hunter has taken many birds with shotgun and bow and recent history has him using his bow exclusively. Jeff still intended to use his bow unless a tom came within 10 yards and in that case, he would use the pistol.

On an evening hunt in late April, Jeff set up inside a small southern Michigan woods that bordered a large agricultural field. The first turkeys spotted were in the field and included a big tom attending to a small harem of hens. Jeff called out to the lovesick male with calls from both a box call and a push button call. Even though it was a windy night, the tom responded to every call with thunderous gobbles. The turkeys soon faded out of sight but much to Jeff's delight, the big tom left the uninterested hens and quietly sought out the loud hen in the woods. Jeff saw the bird sneaking toward his decoys, which were only 10 yards from the blind. The trophy tom stood next to the decoys so Jeff chose the handgun over the bow and readied his revolver by aiming at the gobbler's bright red neck. With a slight pull of the trigger, the gun barked and the turkey hit the turf. That's right, a Judge issued the death sentence in the state of Michigan. Imagine that statement hitting the internet taken out of context!

For all we know, Jeff may be the first hunter in Michigan to legally take a turkey with a handgun. Jeff shot this bird on April 28, 2010. Since then he has also taken a rabbit with the handgun during the Battle Creek Sportsman's Club Wild Bunny Bash, which took place February 19, 2011.

According to Wikipedia, this particular gun was named "The Judge" in 2006, when Bob Morrison, Executive Vice President for Taurus, learned that judges in high-crime areas of Miami, Florida, were purchasing the revolver for personal defense in their courtrooms. I wonder if those same judges have used them on gators? I know that Jeff would!

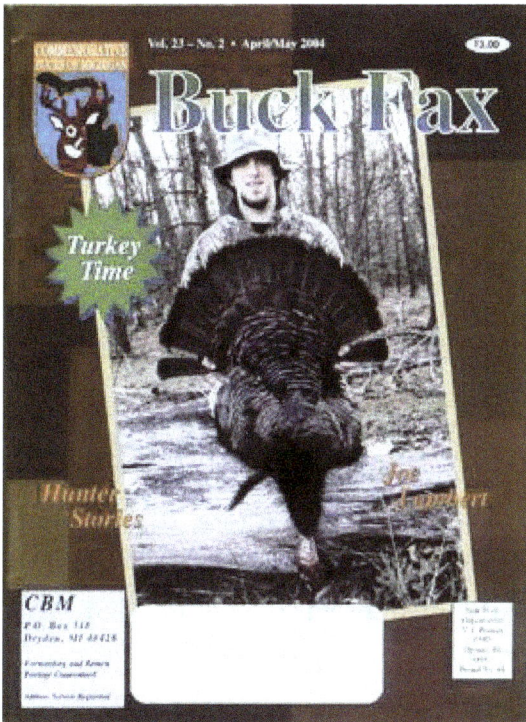

Vol. 23 – No. 2 • April/May 2004 $3.00

COMMEMORATIVE BUCKS OF MICHIGAN

Buck Fax

Turkey Time

Hunter Stories

Joe Lambert

CBM
P O Box 113
Dryden, MI 48428

Ol' Hoppy & Cover Boy

Frustration; I think that this word is applied more to turkey hunting than any other form of hunting. These prehistoric-looking creatures seem to use every molecule of their peanut-sized brain to successfully elude us humans who in theory are supposed to be at the top of the food chain because of our seemingly superior brain power. Turkeys will *hang up* just out of shotgun range, venture off course to thieving hens, spook at our slightest bit of movement or simply go silent and refuse to respond to our calling.

My brother, Joe, was having one of these frustrating seasons a few years back. All of the factors listed above took place, and his season was nearing the end with a lot of hours manned in the woods and no punched tag to show for his efforts. During the last few days of the season, a change of scenery seemed like the ticket for the prevention of insanity.

My other brother, Jeff, had gotten a turkey on opening day so he took Joe to a property where we had seen a lot of turkeys during the previous deer season. This land consisted of woods that bordered a river.

Their first morning there, they heard a lot of gobbling in the distance but only saw a hen. They felt that this property held promise and decided to return the following morning.

The next day, the men got closer to the river and had more action. The birds were gobbling on the roost, and they spotted a couple of nice toms but once again, none came in close enough to shoot. There were now only two days left and they wanted to stick it out on this new piece of property.

On the second to the last day of the season, the hunters woke up even earlier in an attempt to get even further back in the river bottom without scaring any birds off of their roost. However, they were not successful because the birds were roosted closer this time. They decided to back out and set up without the aid of decoys.

Two toms started gobbling back and forth close to their ambush. This was a promising sign, to say the least. They then watched a gobbler fly down and head toward an already landed hen. The hen came into Jeff's calling but the tom, along with his male brother, found a pair of receptive hens and that is when Jeff and Joe noticed the gobbler with the distinctive hop. All four birds went the opposite way including *Ol' Hoppy.*

Jeff took this grand opportunity to harass Joe by commenting, "If you can't shoot a one-legged turkey, then you aren't much of a hunter!"

Joe didn't have a comeback. What can you say when a one-legged turkey eludes you by *hopping* away?!

It now came down to the last day of the season. Jeff and Joe woke up even earlier and made it to where they wanted to set up deep into the thick wet river bottom. At 6:05 a.m., they heard the first gobble followed by double gobbles in the other direction.

They were set up between competing gobblers and felt like they had a good chance of calling in at least one of the three gobblers. After a chorus of one hundred gobbles, the birds went quiet. My brothers concluded that the birds were on the ground, let out a few yelps and then sat waiting. Thirty minutes later, two gobbles rocked the river bottom about sixty five yards away.

After a long hard two weeks of hunting, Joe was getting excited. Jeff was the first to spy one of the birds and Joe quickly spied the other. Joe whispered, "It's Ol' Hoppy." The toms got vocal and Jeff made a few clucks. This got the birds going and they responded with thunderous gobbles echoing throughout the bottom land.

The Ol' tom made his way along a small ridge and Joe was fortunate enough to align him in his sight. A slight tug on the trigger dropped the turkey at forty-five paces. When Jeff and Joe made it to the trophy bird, Joe found out it did have two legs. One was just broken. Joe was extremely pleased to get the bird on the last day of the season. Jeff successfully videotaped the kill and took pictures of the successful hunter.

There are many ways to preserve a turkey hunting memory. You can have a taxidermist mount the entire bird or you can mount the fan, beard and spurs. Some people are happy with a good photograph. Joe sent his photograph and a written story to the Michigan Commemorative Bucks of Michigan magazine, *Buck Fax*. They not only published the story but they placed his picture on the cover.

Ironically, Joe was always clean cut and the first and only year that he grew his hair and beard out, they put him on the cover of a magazine. If you think that we didn't tease him about being a *cover boy* or for the fact that he shot a one-legged turkey, then think again! Joe just attributed it to us being jealous. As far as the bushy beard goes, the bearded Robertson family has been pretty successful with their *Duck and Buck Commander TV* shows. Do they have a *Turkey Commander* yet? Hey, just saying, Jack!

Contagious Enthusiasm

Alan Moore is a passionate man. He likes to take life by the horn and ride it hard. If Al is going to do something, he is going to do it right and do it well. Because of this mindset, there are hundreds of physical therapy patients that are grateful for Al's skill and heartfelt care.

Alan is equally passionate about his hobbies and hunting and fishing top the list. Imagine my good fortune when Al invited me out on a turkey hunt. Any guy that volunteers a new hunting opportunity and place to hunt is indeed a good guy.

I was to meet Alan at a parking lot near his home at 5:15 a.m. I got there at 5:05 a.m. and Al was already waiting for me. Alan jumped out of his truck and said, "I was so excited, I could hardly sleep last night!"

I had hunted unsuccessfully for the full week prior to this morning so Al's contagious enthusiasm was just what the doctor ordered. We entered the woods at 5:50 a.m. At 6 a.m., an owl hooted and a gobbler responded. Al high fived me and was totally geeked with enthusiasm.

The bird was not far off, so we set up in the woods. We placed my decoys into an open lane. Within minutes, there were toms gobbling from three different directions with multiple gobbles resounding from two of the three areas. This was going to be like taking candy from a baby!

Alan was the designated caller and he let out a few soft yelps to let the toms know where to come. At 7 a.m., we saw two hens fly down. By 8 a.m., we had not heard another gobble or seen anything other than the two hens. In other words, we weren't eating the baby's candy!

A little before 9 a.m., Al and I moved out to a hayfield. We found a good set-up area that offered a sweeping view of the rolling field. Utilizing a wooden paddle box call, Al made some soft purring calls. A gobbler immediately answered from another woodlot. The tom was fired up and responded to every call. Shortly thereafter, there were double gobbles and the birds kept getting closer.

After a while, the gobblers sounded like they had held up and were standing their ground. We decided to stop calling and play hard-to-get in hopes that the birds would come looking for us. It worked!

About five minutes later, we heard a loud gobble booming off to our right. A tom entered the field about 150 yards away. When he entered the field, he was in full strut. Soon a second and then a third bird appeared. They were all toms.

A few soft purrs and the trio started coming our way. Their competitive juices started flowing and the three toms began running in our direction. They ran down a tall hill and then sprinted up the smaller hill where we were. They did so at an alarming pace. They were on top of us in no time.

As they drew near, Al was actually laughing under his breath with excitement. I checked all three birds, and they were all sporting long beards. When they got about fifteen yards from the decoys, one of the birds separated from the others, stopped and stuck his head high into the air. At that precise moment, I let loose with a load of three inch Premium five shot from my Remington 11-87. The bird dropped at twenty yards, flapped one wing and then laid still. Al and I exploded with an enthusiastic celebration.

When we bent down to inspect our trophy tom, Al said, "The good Lord blessed us this morning." He surly did.

On the way home, Al verbally replayed our hunt numerous times and was buzzing from his hunter's high. I treated Alan to lunch and thanked him for taking me hunting. Since then, I have taken him deer hunting and we have hunted pheasants. Each outing is an exhilarating experience. Good friendships and compatible hunting camaraderie are treasures to hang on to.

Alan is a good man whose life is a living testament of doing the right thing and doing it with exuberant joy. Luke

6:45, *"The good man brings good things out of the good stored up in his heart."* Amen!

Boo Boo, Scar & the Camp Record

Spruce, poplar, pine and rock make up a good portion of the landscape that surrounds my two-baited treestands in the northern wilderness of Ontario, Canada. The locals simply refer to the area as *the bush* and my map names the remote region as Thunder Bay. We are located a couple hundred miles north of the big lake they call *Gitche Gumee*, the greatest of the Great Lakes, Lake Superior.

Northern Canada is a harsh environment, and I will sit all alone in this thick terrain that provides very, very limited visibility in my quest for black bear. Loneliness, boredom, hopeful anticipation and Smoke Jansen are virtually my only companions. Smoke is the main character of a western novel that I occasionally read to pass time.

I am part of a group of nine hunters from southern Michigan who ventured north. My brothers, Jeff and Joe, are also partaking in the hunt, as are six others who are regular customers at Jeff's pro-shop, Indian Creek Archery.

Our outfitter is Ron Smith, owner of *The Bears Den*, and I am half convinced that Ron is half bear himself. His hair and beard are jet black, and he is as moody and ornery as any of the bruins that we are pursuing. The agile outfitter glides through the trees when approaching baits or tracking wounded prey with his red-bone hound, Scar

On our first night, no one from our party got a bear and I was the only one to see one. A bear entered the bait area and immediately turned around and walked directly back out. Ron referred to this as *bumping the bait*. I saw him for only a couple of seconds but he looked to be about a 200-pound bear.

On the second night, I had a yearling bear come into the bait, and he provided entertainment with his juvenile personality. I nicknamed him Boo Boo because he looked young and playful like Yogi's son. Boo Boo gleefully strolled in and looked in my direction without actually looking at me. Content that all was well in that direction, he then went to the entrance trail and poked his head around the corner to see if anyone was coming. Once again, contentment settled into his demeanor and he then proceeded to the bait bucket. Boo Boo popped the lid, grabbed a piece of meat into his mouth and went back into the bush. I could see Boo Boo eating his piece of meat but then he quickly disappeared and another bear came to the bait. This bear stopped broadside and ate something on the ground. I drew back my bow and placed the site pin tight behind the shoulder. When I punched the release, the arrow struck where I aimed and the bruin let out a growl and rolled onto his back. I could see about 10 inches of my 30 inch arrow sticking out and then the bear ran into the thick bush without another sound.

This was my third hunt for black bears and I had finally gotten my bear. I was very confident with my hit and adrenaline pumped through my veins. When I got back to the lodge, I dutifully reported in to Ron and informed him that I put a good shot on what I thought was the bear that had come in the first night. Jeff had a bear come into his bait as well, and he came to full draw but never shot because the bear didn't present a good angle for a lethal hit. Another hunter from our group, Scott Nelson, missed a big bear so the action was definitely heating up.

After everyone had reported in safely, we assembled a tracking team to go retrieve my bear. The moon was three quarters full and excitement filled the starlit night. When we got to the bait site, Ron and Scar took the lead and I attempted to keep up.

There was no blood or hair at the point of impact and none of the immediate trails had any sign either. Scar kept working down a bear trail and Ron eventually found first-blood about 50-60 yards out. Watching Ron slip through the heavy cover while literally being pulled by his big red-bone hound; left me really impressed with both of their skills in trailing wounded bears. You could tell that Ron lived for these moments, and I was fighting hard to "ride shotgun" during their hot pursuit.

What I didn't like was how little sign the bear was leaving. There was not a lot of blood, and what little we did see, was bright red in color with no bubbles or air in the crimson liquid. Over an hour into the search, we continued to follow Scar's talented nose and found small drops of blood. However, the bear never let up and the evidence showed that the shot did not hit vitals and that the bear was not mortally wounded. Nothing brings on heartache to an ethical hunter more than to wound a game animal and not find it. The usually fired up, high-octane bear guide somberly turned to me and stated, "We're not going to find this bear. He's not mortally wounded and he is going to live another day." I agreed with the prognosis and thanked Ron for his diligent search. The one saving grace in this situation was that through the impressive tracking of Ron and Scar, there was ample evidence that we were not leaving a dead bear out in the woods. The bear would continue to live and more than likely fully recover from what looked like a marginal wound. We concluded that I shot under the vitals. Being a novice bear hunter, I did not factor in that the fur on a bear can have about five inches of hair hanging from the bottom and that I should have shot a little higher.

A full moon arrived on the fourth night and the bear activity shut down. Out of the twenty-plus hunters, only one bear was seen and that hunter did not get a shot. The fifth night only one person saw a bear, or as it was bears, and that person proved to be Jeff. Early in Jeff's evening sit, he had a young yearling come into his bait and Jeff elected to pass. The bear was just too small. When the juvenile bear got to the bait bucket, he played with the bucket without taking any food. Jeff got some great photographs of the silly bruin and named him the circus bear because of his clowning behavior.

As the hours piled on, Jeff took out a book to help pass the time. He was reading about dangerous bears when he looked to his left and saw a big fat black bear lumbering across the rock surface toward his bait. Jeff's first thought was "That's a TV bear," meaning that bear is every bit as big as those brutes they shoot on TV. The big bruin paused behind some trees. When the bear slowly moved on, Jeff drew back his Bowtech bow and when his pin centered behind the shoulder, he punched the release and sent the lethal arrow into the broadside bear.

Upon impact, the bear let loose with a mighty growl, hit the ground then crawled into the brush behind the bait then it went down into a slight depression. Jeff could see a tree moving behind the bucket and knew that the bear didn't go far.

Later that night, Jeff reported his shot to Ron and we all pondered on whether we should go and retrieve the bear that night or in the morning. Ron cautioned on the side of safety and declared, "Dead bear at night, dead bear in morning," and decided to wait until the following morning. Jeff hardly slept a wink. He knew of someone who waited until morning after shooting a bear and found only half a bear because the wolves had eaten it.

The next morning, Jeff and I followed Ron and Scar to the bait site. Scar went down into the depression and Jeff was the first to spot his trophy lying dead 15 yards from where he hit it. When Ron saw the bear, he came running out of the depression fist pumping and completely stoked. When Ron had put Jeff onto this bait, he told him, "I don't usually put a hunter at a bait that has already been hunted, but I had a guy from the first week demand to be moved after only sitting here for one and a half hours. I told him there was a big bear at this site and he didn't believe me. I want you to lace this big bear so I can show him when he returns next year!"

Jeff laced the big bear. Ron shouted out, "That's a big boar." When we went to drag the bear up onto the rock surface for pictures, Ron, looking astonished yelled out again, "It's a sow!" The Bears Den has been keeping records of the weights of bears for over 30 years and the sow record had just been beaten the prior week with a sow that weighed 282 pounds. When Jeff's bear was weighed, it tipped the scales at an unbelievable 320 pounds – smashing the old camp record by 32 pounds! How cool is that?

Two other hunters got bears on the very last night. Scott, who had missed the bear with his bow on the second night put in a marathon eight-hour sit and was duly rewarded when a bear came at 5 pm. Seventeen year old, Dakota Barnes hadn't seen a bear all week but nevertheless stayed positive and killed one in the last minutes of his sit.

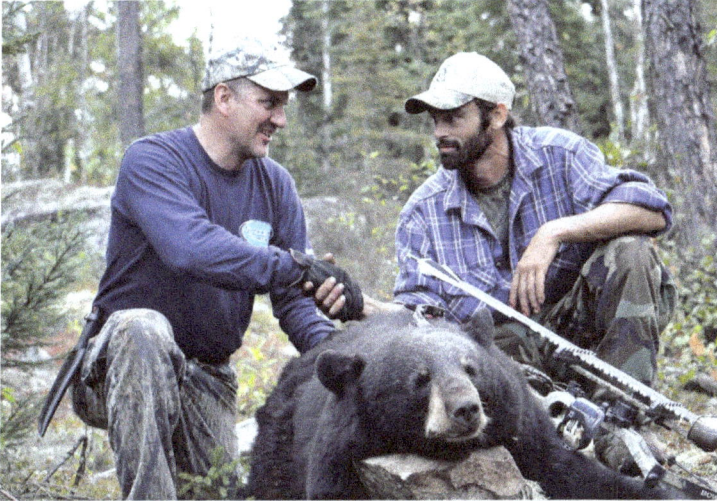

Black bear hunting is often described as hours of complete boredom followed with minutes of exhilarating excitement. This proved to be the case for our bear camp in 2012. As we were retrieving Scott's bear, Jeff said, "When I shot my camp record bear..." He didn't have to say anything else; we all started cracking up. Once again, I didn't get a bear but the whole camp experience lets you bask in the success of others. Scott told us that the bear he shot would weigh at least 250 pounds. Once we got it back at camp, it weighed in at just over 100 pounds. Scott mentioned that he was going to get a wall mount. Naturally, a big group of men at a remote camp couldn't resist razzing him. "Yea, a mount would be nice or you could get a wallet made!" Scott laughed right along with the group and why not, he was going home with his first bear. We all know that bears are the hardest animal in the wildlife kingdom to judge in the field. Every man who made a joke at Scott's expense also shook his hand and congratulated him on getting his first bear. That is bear camp in a nutshell. If you want to leave the politically correct civilized world behind, book a wilderness black bear hunt. It will cleanse your soul!

(According to Canadian officials, Jeff's bear was 17 years old!)

Courageous Girl!

Jessica Olmstead lives in Battle Creek, Michigan, and by most accounts enjoys an active lifestyle. She is athletic, plays softball and has a black belt in Oki Na Wan – Uechiryu, a discipline of Karate. In Karate, she has three Michigan state titles and once took silver in a National's event in Utah. She enjoys partaking in this activity with her mother, Ayumi.

In August of 2010, seventeen year old Jessica chose to engage in her father, Tim's, favorite activity and travel with him to Ontario, Canada, to participate in a bear hunt. The father and daughter duo went hunting with Oba Outfitters, a camp in which Tim had successfully taken bears in the past.

Jessica had never shot a big game animal but enjoyed archery shooting with her Matthews Passion compound bow. On August 23, the two hunters were perched together about fifteen feet high overlooking a bait pile deep into the Canadian wilderness. Their sit proved to be quite eventful as several different bears visited the bait site. One bear in particular caught the young huntress' attention. According to Tim, this particular bear weighed around 300 pounds and possessed a distinctive brown nose. This bear had not presented a shot when it first visited the bait, and Jessica patiently waited for the Mr. Brown Nose to return.

The seventh bear to come to the bait that night was a lone cub. While this little bear lingered at the site and ate, Tim saw a big bear coming across a nearby clearcut. The cub soon noticed this bigger bear, and let out a scream then quickly scampered up a tree. When the big bear arrived, he rose up onto his hind legs and violently shook the tree in an attempt to get the smaller bear to fall. Tim thought to himself at this moment, "I have never seen anything like this. Jessica is having an incredible first hunt."

The boar eventually left the tree and swaggered to the bait but kept his eyes focused on the treed cub. Jessica remained calm and took this opportunity to draw her bow and take aim at the broadside bear. The huge bruin was only sixteen yards from the teenage girl when she released an arrow that struck the bear right behind the shoulder. The bear ran thirty yards and fell over dead for a fast humane kill. Jessica immediately started to shake all over as adrenaline rushed through her body. At this moment, she could not believe how exhilarating this event made her feel.

Shortly thereafter, Jessica and Tim were kneeling beside the monster bear and marveling at its sheer beauty. With assistance from the outfitters, the extra-large bruin was taken back to camp where it was weighed in at an astonishing 448 pounds!

The next morning, pictures were taken and an adventurous memory was preserved that the father and daughter team actively enjoyed together. When the hunters returned home, Tim did what many proud fathers would do. He sent the successful hunter photograph of Jessica and her bear to the hometown newspaper hoping that they would include it in their Sunday outdoor page. Instead, Aaron D. Harris, a reporter from the *Battle Creek Enquirer,* called them and asked to do a feature story.

Well, the story was printed on September 28, 2010, and soon thereafter the Associated Press picked it up and it ran across the nation and Canada. The Olmsteads were receiving calls from Detroit, Cleveland and Toronto. Jessica's story was *on Yahoo Sports, The Bob & Tom Radio Show and The Howard Stern Show*. Soon thereafter, CBS called and scheduled a flight for the Olmsteads to fly to New York to appear on *"The Morning Show."* However, this appointment was cancelled two hours before flight because of breaking national news. She did however, do a live interview for a radio show in Ontario. The wave of publicity was quite a ride!

During this week of media chaos, the Olmsteads googled Jessica's name and had an amazing 315,000 hits. Unfortunately, all of this positive attention soon led to negative attention as well. People from Germany and all over Europe started messaging her facebook account and many of these messages contained statements wishing that Jessica was dead instead of the bear. A lunatic from California took the liberty of writing a letter addressed to Jessica's school with a death threat attached. Sick, cowardly, people were out there hiding behind computers attacking an active, happy, family-orientated high school girl.

Fortunately for Jessica, she has been raised by grounded, sensible parents and the family is not letting the poisonous hate of a few animal-rights zealots impact their positive attitudes or active lifestyles. Jessica's mother stated, "During this wave of negativity, her friends and school teachers have been very supportive and strengthened her."

Harper Creek High School teacher Mike Rio said, "Jessica is a nice girl and her story has been well received at school. It's too bad that people have to attack a nice high school girl because they themselves are ignorant."

I am happy to report that through it all, young Jessica is standing tall. She looked me in the eye and said, "This was a trip that I took with my dad, an experience of a lifetime and I loved it. It really hurt me that people would say such bad things about me. I eat wild game and also have eaten meat from my bear. I participate in deer hunting and will eat the venison if I get a deer. I see hunting as a family orientated activity and a great way of enjoying nature."

I couldn't agree more. Jessica is a courageous girl who stood steady with a massive bear sixteen yards away and has remained equally steady as the beast of hate attempted to rock her world. Happy hunting Jessica, your integrity is inspiring!

Outdoor Ambassadors

Like Billy Graham behind a pulpit or Clint Eastwood in a Cinematic Western, Rick Dosh is definitely a man in his element when he is outdoors amongst the northern Canadian wilderness. Mr. Rick has been traveling from his

Cereal City home (Battle Creek, MI) for thirty-three years to the Mississagi Valley region of Ontario.

Mr. Dosh's daily attire is camouflage and khaki's, accessorized with an assortment of boots and hats that all scream, "I belong here!" Rick often looks like a game warden, and he speaks of people throwing fish from their boats when he has approached them in his boat while on the water.

The fifty-three year old has a grey beard that sets up camp under sparkling green eyes, which display his full joy whenever he steps into the environment that he loves. Dosh's truck has a vanity plate that reads RIMFIRE for his love of guns but his look simply states *a man of the outdoors*.

Every summer, Dosh enjoys three to four weeks of the northern wonderland with his wife, Becky, and their teenage son, Austin. The Doshs spend most days riding their ATVs down the logging roads and trails to beautiful mountain vistas and cascading waterfalls. Pit stops along the way include wild berry picking and viewing wildlife. This Christian family also enjoys boating, canoeing, fishing and swimming a chain of lakes with cold, clear waters.

Although Rick has taken numerous fish, and shot black bear in this wilderness environment, these are not the accomplishments that put the sparkle in his eyes. Rick takes great pride and joy in sharing his piece of paradise with others. Over the years, Rick and his family have hosted over one hundred and fifty people. I had the good fortune of joining in the Christian fellowship after I married my wife, Michelle.

Michelle and her two children, Noah and Lindsey, had ventured up to Canada when the Doshs gave the then single mother of two, a golden opportunity to partake in the foreign world of the great outdoors. They loved it and couldn't wait to introduce me to their new experience. The week before we arrived, one of the other guests picked this spectacular location to propose to his girlfriend. She said, "YES!"

On our trip, the main activity was riding miles of mountain trails on ATVs. The Doshs have bought and maintained a fleet of these machines for the express purpose of sharing with others. Most of the time, Mr. Rick would lead our convoy with Ms. Becky supervising from the rear. Everyday Mr. Rick would lead us down a barely visible trail that would deliver us to either beautiful waterfalls or the summit of a mountain with a grand view. We would then enjoy our packed lunches and capture awesome pictures that we will surely enjoy for years to come.

Ten year old Noah loved trail blazing on the ATVs and seven year old Lindsey indulged in daily feasts of her favorite fruit, blueberries. All of us enjoyed the wildlife viewing and we saw quite an assortment; beaver, fox, wolf, eagles, grouse, rabbits and a Pine Martin. The elusive bear and moose escaped our eyes but we saw plenty of signs that they were around.

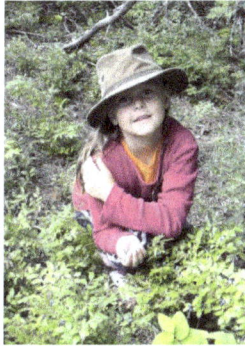

The second afternoon that we were there, Becky took the three children for a half mile swim out to a sandy island in the middle of one of the lakes. This was an amazing adventure and achievement for our ever-growing children. Becky has grown to love the area through her photographer's eye. She has developed such a strong chemistry with her husband that he knows when and where she will ride in front of the group and take pictures of the convoy in areas that offer spectacular backgrounds. Ms. Becky then provides the guests with copies of her photographs so that the memories continue. Her gourmet cooking is on the same level of excellence as her photography. We all kidded that we would have to be rolled back across the Mackinac Bridge.

The Dosh family are true ambassadors of the outdoors and adhere to the Christian principle of "It is better to give than to receive." Through their generosity and kindness, many lives have been greatly enhanced. We may not all be preachers and teachers but we do all hold special gifts that can greatly bless others.

Two years later, I returned to this outdoor paradise with two novice bear hunters and had the grand opportunity of paying it forward. My brother, Joe, and one of our softball playing teammates, Ed, got to see their first wild black bears and enjoyed riding quads to the scenic bait sights. Ed shot a bear about mid-week and now has a rug adorning a wall in his home that serves as a reminder of his successful hunt. Most of us got involved in hunting through the mentoring of a family member or friend, and it is a privilege when we can return the favor to others.

Romans 12:6-8 states, "We have different gifts, according to the grace given us. If a man's gift is prophesying, let him use it in proportion to his faith. If it is serving, let him serve, if it is teaching, let him teach; if it is encouraging, let him encourage, if it is contributing to the needs of others, let him give generously; if it is leadership, let him govern diligently; if it is showing mercy, let him do it cheerfully.

First Peter 4:10 states, "Each one should use whatever spiritual gift he has received to serve others, faithfully administering God's grace in its various forms."

As I look through our family photo album, my senses come alive. I taste fresh berries and then feel the wind as I ride. My eyes feast on the glorious sight of rushing water crashing over the falls, and I feel the cool mist refreshing my skin. I see soaring eagles and a white-coated wolf casually walking the rock bed of a calm wilderness creek. Because of one family's giving heart, my own family now knows about the Canadian wilderness. What a wonderful gift. Thanks for sharing!

My Trophy White Tale

My anticipation level was sky high as I quietly crossed the calf-high creek with a loaded Remington 12-gauge. One hour earlier, I had taken a shot at a big buck that was standing broadside 115 yards from my stand, and I did not know if I had hit him or not. After the shot, he took a couple of bounds further north and then disappeared into the thick cover. I walked along the embankment and saw what I was looking for; bubbly blood, sprayed on top of the waist high weeds. My heart pumped a strong beat within my chest and my spirit jumped with joy. Experience has taught me that not only did my one shot connect but that it had hit the buck's lungs. At the end of the trail should lie a much-desired trophy. I cautiously advanced into a section of chest-high swamp grass searching for the ultimate prize.

This same exact scene played out twenty-five years

earlier when I shot my all-time biggest buck. On November 15, 1986, I was hunting an overgrown lake bottom when I shot at an ultra-wide giant that was standing broadside forty-five yards away. After the shot, the buck turned and bounded away into a thicket of brush. On that day, I was also unsure of a hit until I walked to where the buck was standing and saw the yellow marsh grass covered in bright red blood. When I followed the crimson highway, it led me to a tall-tined, 12-pointer that sported an incredible 20 ½ inch, inside spread.

Now it is 2011, twenty-five years later and I am still living the whitetail dream. In September, I released my first book, *Trophy White Tales: A classic collection of campfire stories about North America's #1 game animal - the whitetail deer.* On the front cover, there is a painting of my 1986 trophy. A lot of time and effort went into the writing, editing, formatting and marketing of the book including exciting interviews on *Michigan Out-of-Doors TV, Q1 Buck Pole TV* and *Mike Avery's Outdoor Magazine Radio Show.* Time alone in the woods has been very rewarding following a incredibly busy year. Bow season was unusually warm, windy and abnormally slow compared to most years. I did have a close encounter with a 20 inch, 9-pointer, but I entered the gun season without punching a tag.

When the Michigan gun season opened on November 15, I chose to hunt a tripod stand that sits right in the middle of one hundred acres that I own with my brother, Jeff. This property is an overgrown pasture filled with a wide variety of trees and shrubs that possess sharp thorns. If you have ever hunted plains game in Africa, this property matches it with the biting projectiles. I personally find it beautiful because deer love the security that this kind of cover has to offer.

A heavy fog engulfed southern Michigan for the first three hours of the opener, and I only saw one deer during that time period. Shortly after 10 a.m., the fog lifted and I saw a deer's head reflecting sunlight in the thick cover to the north. However, it vanished within seconds and I could not identify whether it was a buck or doe.

Around 11:30, I felt the wind shift from the southwest to the east, and I knew that I had to find a new location. I decided to hunt a different property that had an ideal stand for this particular wind. Before leaving, I took a handsaw out of my backpack and cut down a six-inch diameter tree that was in the way of shooting deer to the north. I knew that I would be returning here at a later time and wanted to have every option available.

At 2 p.m., I relocated to a classic set-up. I had a hang-on stand placed in the middle of a cluster of four maple trees that shared a common trunk. At 5 p.m., I looked to the south and saw a buck standing about forty yards away. Branches obstructed my view of his rack, but I prepared for a possible shot. He eventually turned and I could see his left side. He carried a tall white rack with at least three standing. I aligned him in my scope and pulled the trigger. He gingerly ran through the woods, stopped about seventy-five yards away and a second slug anchored him to the turf. This buck turned out to be a tall 8-pointer that resembled one that I arrowed the previous year and is featured in *Trophy White Tales* under the chapter titled,

White Pine, Black Water, A treestand perspective of the Kalamazoo River Oil Spill.

With one buck down, I now wanted to focus my attention on the other property, where I had an encounter with the wide 9-pointer. I had captured two pictures of a wide 8-pointer whose antlers sat on top of a very large bodied deer. The first picture of this great buck shows him standing broadside with his head turned looking directly at the camera. From a photographer's viewpoint, it is absolutely the best picture that I have ever snapped. The heavy brute is standing in water with sunlight reflecting off of him. The picture reminded me of the great 12-pointer from 1986 because he also was standing broadside and looking at me from a similar habitat.

On November 17, 2011, I returned to the tri-pod stand that I was sitting in on opening day. It was a cold frosty morning with a light breeze out of the southwest. Clouds covered the sky and snow would occasionally fall. At 8:47, I looked to the north and saw a heavy-horned buck walking toward the thicket that I had named *The Sanctuary*. I quickly placed my Remington 1100, 12-gauge on my shooting stick and turned in my seat for the shot. Fortunately, the buck stopped and looked toward me. He was standing just like the large 8-point from the picture and like the 12-point did twenty-five years prior. I knew that he was about 100 yards away and quickly cranked the variable scope up to a higher setting. I then placed the cross hairs behind his shoulder and pulled the trigger.

He took a couple of bounds further north and disappeared. Buck fever hit and I started to shake. Did I hit him? Please Lord, I hope so. One long hour later, I was standing where the big buck was when I shot as outlined in the beginning of this story. I found the precious bubbly red blood sprayed on the grass. I cautiously followed the blood trail through chest high swamp grass just like I did twenty-five years ago. About one-hundred yards later, I found the thick wide-antlered buck laying atop a bunch of thorns with bubbly red blood outlining a hole in the middle of his body. He was the large bodied 8-point that posed for the trail camera. Field dressing would reveal a perfect double-lung hit. I was thankful that I had taken the time to shoot before the season at one-hundred yards and that I had cut the tree down on opening day, which allowed for a clear shot.

My brother, Joe, agreed to come to my aid and help me drag the brute through the thicket across the creek and up a steep embankment. After field dressing the buck, I returned to my truck to find Joe waiting on me. As it turned out, Joe had to wait another half hour because I was scheduled to do a phone interview with Duran Martinez from the *Wild Michigan Outdoors Radio Show*. I interviewed with Duran from the cab of my truck while I had a big buck down two hundred yards away. How cool was that?

I really love the aesthetics of deer hunting. To be blessed with such a beautiful trail camera picture of this magnificent buck on property that I own is very special. To shoot this trophy as he travels through wonderful whitetail habitat with a very well placed shot is a true joy. I would like to extend a special salute to all my family and friends who contribute to making my hunter life so special. I also want to thank all of the faithful readers who continually seek out my work. I hope you have your very own Trophy White Tale in the near future!

Lessons Learned

For the Picketts family, the 2009 Michigan deer season was becoming a banner year. Guy Picketts, Sr. along with his two sons, Guy Jr. and Matt, had tagged four good bucks and two does. At the end of the November shotgun season, Guy Sr. had seen a giant buck and was anxiously awaiting the upcoming muzzleloader season in December. Unfortunately, bad news put a halt to these plans when the elder Pickett was diagnosed with pancreatic cancer. The close-knit family was devastated and found the news hard to accept since Guy Sr. was in such good shape and had no physical signs of illness. The doctor's prognosis was grim but the former deputy detective was determined to fight.

The following spring found the Picketts men afield once again; this time in pursuit of the old long beard. Guy

Sr. shot a big tom on opening day and called in another for a good friend. On the second day of the season, Senior called in a long beard for Junior. After the shot, the successful tag-team became quite emotional when the grim reality of the situation hit them that this was more than likely their last turkey hunt together.

Guy Sr. continued to fight the war against cancer and became optimistic as fall slowly came back around. Once again, Senior planned on accompanying his sons during the November 15th firearm opener. The boys took part in the early archery season and kept their father informed of the various bucks sighted. Senior told his sons that one of the two of them was going to get a big buck that year. Sometimes you just know and Senior spoke this with absolute faith.

On November 2, Guy Jr., arrowed a nice buck that looked like at least an 8-pointer. Guy thought that he had made a good shot so he enlisted the help of his brother and took to tracking after waiting a couple of hours. Initially, they had a good blood trail, but it quickly faded and there was no sign of a lung hit so they backed out. The brothers then went to their mentor's home and talked the situation over with their father. Guy Sr. said that it was cold and no rain was in the forecast so it would not hurt to leave the buck alone and return the following day.

At first light the anxious hunter was back on the track. Little brother had to work, so dad offered to help. Guy Jr. knew his father wasn't feeling well so he told him that he would call if assistance was needed. The buck had crossed onto a neighboring property so Guy got permission to continue his search and the landowner even offered to help. The blood trail soon faded away, and the two men attempted to spread out in hopes of finding the buck dead. Guy Sr. made several calls and eventually he advised his son to return to last blood and slow down. He told Guy to take a good look around and to make sure that he hadn't missed anything.

Guy Jr. did as he was told and was soon rewarded with finding his buck under a small downfall that the buck had crawled up under. Guy immediately called his father and told him the good news. Guy commented, "Dad was so excited that you would think that he had shot the buck!"

Guy Sr. knew that there was a long drag to get the buck out, so he immediately offered to help. Guy Jr. wisely declined. Well, the drag was indeed difficult and Guy Jr. kept hearing his phone ring but stayed on task and got the buck back to an area in which he could retrieve it with his truck. As the successful hunter crested a hill, he looked up and there stood Dad in his plaid wool coat and rubber boots. He asked his son what took so long and added that he was worried because he had not heard from him. Guy Jr. knew that the truth was that his dad was just too excited and couldn't wait for his son to bring the deer by his house.

The two men loaded the deer up into the truck and then stayed out in the field and talked for about an hour. Guy Sr. told his son that he was proud of him for not giving up and locating the downed buck. Even though the buck was not as big as Guy Jr. thought it was, it was still a nice 9-point and Guy Sr. reminded his son that any deer taken with a bow is a trophy. Guy Jr. noticed that his dad didn't actually say anything out of the ordinary, but he made sure to reiterate his points more than normal. As is his habit, dad made sure that the deer was properly tagged.

Shortly after getting the deer home and hung in the garage, Guy received another call from his dad. They enjoyed another short conversation and Guy Sr. finished by telling his son that he would call once more before Guy Jr. went to work.

Two hours later, Guy's phone rang again and it turned out to be the worst phone call of his young life. Guy Sr. had passed away comfortably at home while sitting on the couch. Guy Sr. had fought the cancer all the way up till the end but his body finally had enough.

Naturally, the next few days were a blur for the Picketts as anyone who has been there can confirm. The overwhelming nature of such an event is draining. The day after the funeral, November 7, Guy Jr. and his brother were at their mother's house just trying to catch their breath. They jointly decided that they needed some fresh air, and it would be a good day to take off for an afternoon bowhunt. That very afternoon, Guy Jr. ended up shooting his all-time biggest buck. The shot that he made was his best ever. The arrow clipped the heart and the buck only went twenty-five yards. When the buck went down, Guy thanked his dad. Guy instantly thought about how his dad had told him that he was going to get a big buck, and he believes that his dad led this buck to him. Another way to look at it would be that his dad led Guy to the buck with a lifetime of *lessons learned*.

When sharing this story, Guy Jr. commented, "My dad worked hard his whole life, but he was never too busy to take my brother and I out hunting. From the time I could walk, my dad and I were spending time in the field pursuing small and big game. My dad taught me pretty much all I know about hunting and life. My brother and I do our best to get our kids out in the woods to spend time and pass on all the things our dad taught us. Thanks for everything, dad!"

Photo Courtesy of Guy Picketts Jr.

Twin Towers

Bob Reits' world literally came crashing down in the spring of 2007. The third generation fireman fell off a ladder while fighting a fire and broke his knee. Three surgeries later and it was time for physical therapy and intensive rehabilitation.

With lots of extra time on his hands, Bob chose to scout for deer around his parent's home, which is located in Paw Paw, Michigan. In late August, Bob's eyes took in a delightful sight. Feeding in a soybean field was an absolute monster of a buck with extremely tall thick antlers and countless points. Reits nicknamed the trophy buck, *Twin Towers* based on the impressive dimensions of this world-class whitetail. Reits developed a burning desire to get this exceptional buck in the coming season.

Fortunately for Bob, his physical therapist was a bowhunter and after much thought, the therapist recommended a climbing treestand. He felt that this type of stand would best suit his patient's needs. Reits chose a Summit Viper and quickly fell in love with the stand.

Bob hunted almost every morning and evening during the month of October. He stated that he constantly moved from tree to tree on the two-hundred acre parcel that he hunted. Reits was determined in his pursuit and passed up smaller bucks in hopes that his desired trophy would appear.

On October 25, it was a sunny sixty-plus degree day and a full moon was scheduled for the coming night; not exactly ideal conditions for deer hunting. Nonetheless, Reits continued his quest. On this evening sit, the bowhunter chose a forked tree in some river bottom habitat. He positioned his stand twenty feet up the left trunk and utilized the right trunk for cover. He faced the stand towards a thicket. Shortly after sunset, Bob finally saw *Twin Towers* while afield. Unbelievably, the trophy was approaching the bowhunter's shooting area. Bob drew his bow back a couple of minutes before the buck came into the opening. He could clearly see the rack approaching through the brush.

When the mighty buck reached the opening, he was only twenty yards away. Bob dumped the string on his seventy-pound Mathews bow and placed his arrow right behind the deer's shoulder. He watched the heavy-horned brute run off with his arrow lodged in him.

Bob did not see the buck go down so he enlisted some help in tracking. Joining Bob was his girlfriend, Jess, his brother, Daniel, and friends, Gary and Brandon. They were all aware that Reits had been pursuing this specific buck so they were almost as anxious as he was to find it.

After a short eighty-yard trail, they found the Michigan Monster. Bob's arrow effectively took out both lungs. Bob stated that he was so excited that he was "screaming like a girl." The tracking party commenced to celebrating!

Reits phoned several of his friends while he was out in the field and when he arrived home, there were a lot of trucks in his driveway waiting for him. What everyone got to see was an incredible 11 by 8, 19-point buck. This world-class buck scored 205 non-typical Boone and Crockett points. He was a seven and a half year old that weighed 207 pounds field dressed.

Reits' previous best was a 215 pound 10-point that he took with a shotgun. Bob states that he has averaged one buck a year for the last sixteen years but has never taken anything of this caliber. Bob described this particular pursuit as "the most exciting hunt I've ever had."

Talk about turning lemons into lemonade. The injured firefighter made the most of his tragic situation and tagged the buck of his dreams. Instead of feeling sorry for himself, Bob Reits pushed hard through rehab and made the most of his time away from work. *Twin Towers* is truly a buck of a lifetime!

Man's Best Friend

In the hunter's dictionary, heartbreak is defined as an empty blood trail. Shooting an animal and then not recovering it after an extensive long search, churns the stomach of the ethical, conscientious hunter.

Bad shots happen to even the best of shooters. A variance of an inch can sometimes make a huge difference in how effective the projectile will kill and also how fast. Sometimes even *perfect* shots do not provide desired sign.

In 2009, I successfully placed a Rage broadhead through both lungs of a broadside doe. I watched as she sprinted one hundred and fifty yards across a soybean field into a wooded fence line. I went to where I last saw her and found mere specs of blood. A very sparse blood trail traveled another hundred yards. When I found the doe piled up beside a barb-wired fence, my initial observations were correct. The arrow passed through both lungs. So how did she go far and leave so little sign? Well, these animals are unbelievably tough. In this case, a large chunk of fat covered the exit hole. In reality, the deer was only alive for a few seconds after the shot but covered a lot of ground during her death run.

A couple of weeks later, my brother, Joe, put the same shot on an 8-point buck. Once again, the deer took off on a dead sprint and we followed only flecks of blood. We totally lost all sign of blood when the buck crossed a cut soybean field. Fortunately for us, we were quite familiar with the property and after a couple of hours of searching, I walked up on the dead buck. This time the arrow had remained in the deer and plugged the entrance hole. This big buck ran over three hundred yards before giving up the spirit.

These scenarios could have had vastly different outcomes for less experienced trackers or if we were hunting unfamiliar properties. Truth is, not all mortally hit game leaves behind a visual blood trail. Leaving a dead game animal in the wild is unacceptable to the conscientious hunter. So what is a person to do?

I am a firm believer that every problem has a solution. One answer that is gaining popularity is the use of *blood tracking hounds*. Training a dog in this age-old tradition is one option or calling upon a business that specializes in this service is also a possibility. In my home state of Michigan, a hound-handler by the name of Rob Miller received so many requests from his friends and family that he saw a need and began a successful small business called Michigan Deer Track'n Hounds. Helping discouraged hunters find their *lost* game is an exciting adventure that Rob and his fellow dog-men immensely enjoy.

On November 11, 2012, crossbow hunter, Joe Alongi, shot a wide-antlered buck. Joe thought that the shot looked good and watched the buck wobble as it walked away. Alongi commented, "I could see the arrow sticking out of him with blood pouring out. I waited a half hour and then climbed down from my stand."

Joe recruited his father and two friends to help blood trail the wounded buck. They followed good blood for about two hundred yards and then it became very sporadic with just small specs. At this point, Joe elected to back out and get a tracking dog.

Alongi phoned Michigan Deer Track'n Hounds and Rob agreed to meet him the following morning. Joe and his tracking team spent hours tracking the day before. Rob's hound, Sypris, covered the half mile distance in about twenty minutes. When the dog got to where Joe had lost blood, he made a wide loop and found the buck completely hidden within a thick briar patch of wild rose.

Photo Courtesy of Joe Alongi

Twenty four hours after the deer was shot, Joe got to put his hands on the 160-class, 11-point. Alongi was extremely happy and commented, "That dog was awesome. It was amazing what he could do. I never would have found my buck without the help of the dog."

Joel Ruggles completely agrees and has his own testimony to tell. The bowhunter shot a big buck that stood broadside at twenty-five yards. Upon being hit, the big buck ran off into a nearby swamp. After dark, Joel started trailing the buck with the help of his brother, John, and good friend, Scott. As the men began their search, it started to rain. Initially there was a good blood trail and this remained true for the first two-hundred yards. As the rain continued to fall, the trail came to an abrupt end.

Scott brought on new hope when he suggested calling his friend who has a tracking dog. Joel asked, "How much would it cost?"

Scott replied, "One hundred dollars. Is this deer worth one hundred dollars to you?" Without hesitation, Joel responded a definite, "Yes!"

Scott soon got ahold of Mike Riepen who works for Michigan Deer Track'n Hounds. Mike loaded up his hound, *Cash*, and met the men at the scene.

When Mike put Cash on the trail, he easily covered the first couple hundred yards. When they reached the spot where the men had lost the trail, Cash took a direct turn and they started to once again find blood. The trail then went into some tall grasses but then the blood sign stopped. Cash took them through the tall marsh grass and into an open field. With absolutely no sign of blood, Mike doubted Cash and restarted him at last blood. Once again, Cash wanted to cross the large open field so Mike let Cash do his thing. When they got to the other side, Mike asked Joel to look for blood. It was at this spot the two men discovered more blood. A steady blood trail returned and the men followed Cash up a hill where sure enough, they found the big buck.

Cash successfully trailed the wounded buck 1.8 miles. Even though the shot had appeared to be properly placed, in reality Joel had gut-shot the deer. The buck carried 13 points and scored 164 Pope and Young points.

Joel reflected on Mike and Cash's successful tracking job, "It was really amazing, I had never seen a dog track before. *Cash* was more than worth the cash money spent.

There is no way that we would have found my deer without that dog!"

Blood tracking hounds have proven to be an incredible asset to hunters and can eliminate the dreadful experience of losing mortally hit game. Joe and Joel each have their respective *buck of a lifetime* thanks to the incredible abilities of blood tracking hounds. Once again, dogs prove to be man's best friend!

Photo Courtesy of Joel Ruggles

Take a Walk on the Wild Side!

A deer trail the size of a cattle run was grooved through the side of a hill, which was covered, with an assortment of pine and spruce trees. My family and I had planted them a few years prior. The taller ones were just now reaching my six-foot height. This area had developed into an occasional bedding area for the resident deer herd, and I was eager to hunt my way through the cover with high hopes of surprising a buck on his own turf.

I walked into the wind, which was blowing out of the west. My eyes scanned the habitat of tall grass and conifer trees. I carefully placed each step quietly onto the path and then would scan my surroundings from this fresh new perspective and view. Halfway across the hill, I saw what I was looking for. An antlered buck was standing forty yards away sloped slightly uphill from my position. Only his head was visible in the tall grass so I placed the iron sights of my 12-gauge shotgun on the visible target and pulled the trigger. He dropped where he stood. This hunt happened many moons ago, but it was an exciting adventure to tag a buck that I beat in the security of his own living space.

A few years later, my brother, Jeff, and I bought a one-hundred acre property that consisted of overgrown pastureland. At that time, there were less than ten trees in which we could place a treestand, and the rest of the landscape consisted of high feral grass and a variety of shrubs and brush. The archery season came and went without any opportunities for shooting a buck.

At that time, it was unlawful to hunt from an elevated position with a firearm so we were forced to hunt from the ground, which offered very limited visibility due to the high grass and shrubs. After a week of unsuccessful firearm hunting, we decided to conduct a *deer drive* on Thanksgiving Day. I would be the stander on the first drive and Jeff was going to *push* a patch of brush on the northern part of the property. When Jeff was walking toward his starting point, a buck jumped from the grass and he snap-shot it in a fashion that would make any rabbit hunter proud. This was Jeff's first buck while afoot, and he was quite happy with his accomplishment.

The following day, I chose to purposely sleep in and conduct a mid-day still-hunt diagonally across our one-hundred acre parcel like the frontiersmen had done in the early 1700s. With the wind in my face, I started my hunt in a brush-choked marsh that had lots of deer sign. Very slowly, I advanced through the habitat by following one of the many deer trails. I found several beds and rubs but no deer were dwelling there that day. I then slipped up to slightly higher ground and weaved through head-high bushes. When I poked through the shrubs into a grassy opening, I stopped and scanned the landscape. Once again, I observed the head and this time neck of a whitetail buck. This buck was standing in the tall grass and looking in my direction at a distance of one-hundred yards. I placed the crosshairs of my scope on the white patch of his throat and fired the 12-gauge. This buck also dropped in his tracks. I cautiously approached the area where he disappeared and found him lying in the tall grass. The buck only had one antler but that one antler turned out to be rather impressive and carried six points. After a long season of unsuccessful stand hunting, this was a rewarding endeavor.

It's no secret that stand hunting is the most productive method for consistently taking deer and is by far the best method for taking mature animals. Still-hunting stacks the deck in favor of the whitetail, but when the hunter breaks the odds and comes out on top, it is all that much *sweeter.*

A few years later, my brother, Joe, and I chose to do a two-man still-hunt through some tall grass on a cold morning in which the sky was dumping a mix of snow and sleet. This habitat offered ideal cover for the ring-neck pheasants that lived in the area. Big bucks also coveted the cover and would lay up in the grass, so we intended to slowly cover the land in the same method that we would hunt pheasants. Sure enough, we *flushed* a 10-point buck that I shot through the heart immediately after he jumped from his bed, a mere 20 yards away from where I was standing. We made the best out of a bad weather day and also made a great memory!

This past year, Epizootic Hemorrhagic Disease (EHD) hammered our region killing thousands of deer. I entered the season with very low expectations due to the massive die-off. Fortunately, I am able to hunt multiple properties and on one of the parcels there was limited die offs. Unfortunately, it did take out the two biggest bucks that we had game camera photographs of; a tall-tined 8-point and a 160-class 14-point that we had high hopes of tagging.

There were only two bucks left on the property that I would guess to be over three and half years old. The cover was thick so getting a good look at them proved to be difficult. On the second morning of gun season, I saw what I thought was a high-horned 8-point chasing a doe. The following day, I went out for an afternoon sit in the area where I had seen the buck. I had a tripod stand located in a grove of pines that I had transplanted a few years prior and knew that it would be a good choice for the southeast wind. To get to my stand, I had to walk by a thicket of dogwood whips. A few years back, I had jumped a 3-point buck out of the tangle and knew that this could always happen again. Sure enough, the tall buck that I had seen chasing the doe bounded up and took off running for the woods. Hearing the buck take off out of the cover, I raised my shotgun and took a shot at the running deer that was only forty yards away. I then had to run around some brush for a quick fifteen-yard dash, and I saw the buck stop just inside the woods. I once again raised my gun and took another shot at the stag, which was now about eighty yards away. He took one step behind some trees and brush then disappeared.

A half hour later, I approached the area where he disappeared and found him lying dead on the ground. My first shot had penetrated the vitals; my second shot center punched a tree. The apparent 8-point was actually a short tined 7-point. The buck was later aged at three and a half years old and was one of the heaviest bucks that I had ever taken off this property. The only one to rival it was a trophy 8-pointer that I had taken the year before.

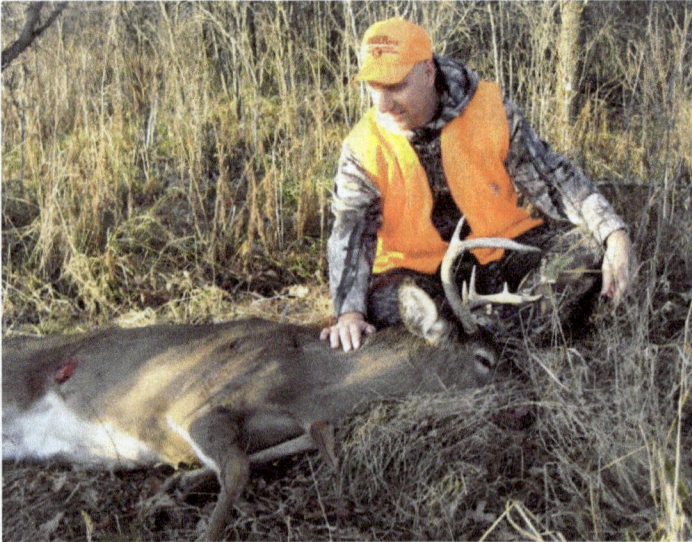

An old cliché' says that there is more than one way to skin a cat. Well, there is more than one way to hunt for deer. Stand hunting will remain the most effective and most often used method for deer hunting but when conditions are right, it's good to step out of the box and try alternative techniques. Pressured deer, especially mature bucks, will often bunker down in heavy cover and become nocturnal. Sometimes you need to go to where they are and *take a walk on the wild side*. I'm glad that I have; the memories are grand!

Lucky

Luck has been a part of hunting since the beginning of time. In the sporting world, there is even an old saying that says, "I'd rather be lucky than good." Successful deer hunters will still accept good luck whenever it's available, but they would rather rely on their own hard work and preparation. Whenever someone successfully takes a trophy caliber buck, they are often referred to as lucky. If someone accomplishes this task on a yearly basis, they are often deemed to be a poacher or *extremely lucky*. What people forget about luck is that it is a two-sided sword. There is good luck, which is thankfully accepted, but there is also bad luck, which usually multiplies with human error.

In my home state of Michigan, one of the best days to experience good luck is on the opening day of gun season. This takes place every year on November 15, and usually coincides with the peak of the rut. I have not missed an opening day hunt since my college years, which was many moons ago. I like to awaken extra early on this magical day to shower, eat breakfast and get to my stand an hour before legal shooting time begins. Imagine my horror when in 2010, I was suddenly awakened by my wife a mere 10 minutes before the first shots could legally be shot. Somehow, in my preparation, I had set my alarm for 4:30 p.m. instead of 4:30 a.m. How lucky was that?

I quickly got dressed, loaded my gear and raced down the highway turning a forty minute drive into a half hour sprint. By the time I had made it to my stand, I had missed a precious forty minutes of prime-time hunting. I was totally disgusted with myself over this amateurish, dreadful rookie mistake.

Unbelievably, I saw more deer that morning than any other opening day that I had ever hunted. In addition, I saw four bucks and two looked to be possible shooters. My hunting partners, brothers, Jeff and Joe, got out an hour before first light and hardly saw any deer. Maybe it is better to be lucky than good!

My action slowed down after 11 a.m., so I decided to meet Jeff and Joe at Jeff's place to eat a quick lunch and formulate a plan for the rest of the day. The wind was forecasted to stay out of the southwest, so I wanted to return to my same stand that I had used during the morning hunt.

Jeff had a stand in an oak tree on the other side of the thicket and a little farther to the north so he wanted to give that spot a try. Joe chose to join us and picked a spot on the northern section of the property that overlooked another thicket.

While we ate lunch, Jeff showed us his latest trail camera photographs from the property. These photographs included a wide 8-point and a small tight-horned 9-pointer. Michigan has a two-buck limit, and Joe and I had already shot good bucks with our bows so we were holding out for a big buck. I had arrowed a 9-pointer in mid-October and Joe had tagged an 8-pointer. For the first time in a very long time, Jeff had not shot anything with his bow prior to the gun season. I knew that his trigger finger would be getting itchy, so I thought that the little 9-point might be in trouble if he came too close to Jeff's stand.

Early in the evening, the deer once again started parading by my stand. A loud shotgun blast came from Jeff's direction. Two more shots rang out. A few moments later, my phone vibrated and I answered with, "What did you shoot?"

Jeff replied, "I think it's the 9-point from the pictures. I know I hit him but I didn't see him go down. He went into the thicket in between us. I am going to get down and look while we still have good light. Be prepared in case he comes out towards you."

I watched Jeff descend from the oak and then the orange vested hunter disappeared as he entered the thicket. A few seconds later I saw a white horned buck come running out of the thicket. My Remington 12-gauge was already placed in the fork of my shooting stick, and I quickly found the running deer in my scope. Apparently, Jeff didn't hit it that well and it was my duty to put the injured animal down. I pulled the trigger and could tell that I hit the running deer. He kept coming my way so I pulled the trigger a second time and nothing happened. The spent shell was jammed in the gun's action. The deer ended up stopping twenty yards in front of me and tipped over.

When it fell to the ground, my phone buzzed again. As I reached for the phone, a disturbing thought came to mind. I answered my phone by asking, "I did just shoot your buck, didn't I?"

Jeff answered, "I don't know what you shot but I'm standing next to the one I shot and it's the 9-point."

I climbed down off of my tripod stand and walked over to the downed buck that I had shot. Lying in the waist high grass was a plump, white-horned, 4-point. I had now limited out on bucks for the year and would not be able to further pursue the big ones including one that I had targeted and named Gnarly. Bad luck had found me twice in one day.

Jeff walked over to me and looked at the small buck then said, "A few years ago, we would have been pretty excited about getting a double." I nodded a silent reply and then my phone vibrated again. It was Joe asking, "What's going on?"

I replied, "We have shot two bucks and recovered them. Keep hunting and maybe you'll get a shot then we will go three for three."

Jeff and I dragged the two lightweights to a small clearing for field dressing. With the two bucks lying side by side, we heard Joe shoot. The wide 8-point had made an appearance and Joe hit him.

We went to help Joe look for his deer. There was a good blood trail but the deer made it onto a neighboring property. We hadn't found any bubbles in the blood, so we decided to take care of the other two bucks and come back for the third one in the morning.

The following morning we secured permission to look for the deer. Around 8 a.m., I found the buck or at least what was left of him. A faint blood trail led me to a steaming gut pile. I looked up from where I was standing and could see the road elevated above me. For years I had heard stories about people finding a gut pile at the end of their tracking but I didn't believe most of these stories. It had finally happened to us. There were no shots from that direction during the prior hour so somebody driving by must have seen it and taken it. How lucky is that?

As fate would have it, our *luck* continued throughout the rest of the shotgun season. I still had a doe tag left. My first night out, who makes an appearance? None other than the previously mentioned, "Gnarly." The magnificent 8-point posed broadside for a full five minutes at one hundred yards and all I could do was watch him!

After dark, I called my two brothers and told them about my encounter and suggested that one of them sit there the next night because I was confident that Gnarly would return. Jeff accepted the offer.

The following night, I was Christmas shopping with my wife when right before dark, my phone rang. I knew that it would be Jeff. Indeed it was and Jeff had just shot "Gnarly". Because Jeff is color blind, I agreed to help him track the big buck.

When I met up with Jeff, he told me his story. "Gnarly" had come into this little waterhole to drink and was facing him. It was getting dark under the canopy of trees so Jeff took the front-on shot expecting to break the big buck's neck and drop him in his tracks. As he told me this, I remembered something from my hunt the night before that I had forgotten to tell Jeff. As "Gnarly" stood broadside, I could make out an unnatural growth protruding from his neck. I shared this with Jeff as we walked, and he remarked that he might have hit the deer there because he had found a slimy substance on the ground where the deer had stood.

Sure enough, there was this mucus slime sprayed in the leaves. I didn't find blood until we were a quite a ways down the trail and the blood was sparse. We trailed the buck for a good half mile without finding any bloody beds or the dead deer and then the trail petered out. Jeff and Joe returned the next morning and after a grid search of the area, came up empty as well.

Injuring an animal and losing it is one of the worst outcomes for a hunter. We found out two years later that Gnarly actually survived the ordeal when he once again showed up on trail camera photographs. He was now at least a 5 ½ year old and carried an even more impressive rack. As fate would have it, the EHD disease struck our region and killed virtually every deer in the area. Once again, luck was not on our side. No more bucks were shot in 2010. Jeff ended up tagging a couple of does.

When the 2011, season rolled around, Jeff chose to hunt the same oak in which he had shot the 9-point from the year before. On the second day of the October archery season, Jeff's luck was about to take an upturn. Once again, a big buck came in at the end of the night. This time, Jeff buried an arrow tight behind the shoulder. This buck was not getting away! Jeff and I found the big buck after a short seventy-yard tracking job. The 11-pointer sported a short drop-tine off the right beam. Jeff always wanted to shoot a drop-tines buck and his dream came true. *Lucky!*

My brothers and I have been rather fortunate in experiencing a fair amount of perceived success on big Michigan bucks. We put in a lot of time and effort and almost every year at least one of us will collect a trophy buck. Sometimes we are lucky and sometimes we are unlucky but overall, we enjoy the chase. If we killed every big buck that we pursued, it would be called shooting instead of hunting. Here's looking forward to many more days afield whether they be *lucky* ones or not!

Photo Courtesy of Rich Schweitzer

"Something Real Good is About to Happen!"

Camaraderie is a word that gets thrown into many stories about deer hunting and for good reason. Deer hunting develops a spirit of fellowship that often bonds those who share in this passionate activity. For Ohio hunter,

Rich Schweitzer, it is much desired time that he spends afield with his brother, Ron, and cousin, Charlie. Charlie drives north from his home in Florida to partake in this annual hunt.

Rich owns three small parcels of land that add up to fifty-one acres in Tuscarawas County, which is located fifteen miles from Canton, the home of the Pro Football Hall of Fame. The terrain is rolling hills of wooded cover. Lots of deer bed on Schweitzer's properties because of the thick multi-flora vegetation and due to a high number of downed treetops felled from earlier logging and mining operations.

On the second day of the Ohio firearm season, Rich was once again afield with his cousin, Charlie. Ron had to work that morning so it was just the two of them. Schweitzer's favorite method of hunting is to still-hunt. He likes to slowly move through the cover and scan his surroundings for deer. To be successful with this method of hunting, a person must discipline himself to move slowly, stay focused and to blend into one's surroundings. On that particular day, there was a light snow falling and Rich described the morning as quiet. The two still-hunters "ran some does out" and decided to move on to another one of Rich's properties.

On the second parcel, the men made a game plan. Charlie was going to sit in the woods along a creek and Rich would slowly work his way through a brush-choked field toward his cousin. Rich states that he turned to walk away and remembered that he forgot to do the customary fist-bump that the men did before each hunt to wish each other good luck. When he turned back around and extended his fist, he told Charlie, "I don't know what it is but something real good is about to happen!" Intuition has blessed many a hunt. Time would tell if this particular premonition would hold true.

A half hour into the hunt, Charlie took a shot and texted Rich, big doe down. Happy for his cousin's success, Rich continued to still-hunt to Charlie's location. Schweitzer had made his way into a thick section of cover when he sensed movement over his left shoulder. When the shotgun-toting hunter turned to look, he saw a big buck working his way slowly down a game trail. Rich said, "I could see a lot of bone and a lot of points."

The deer was one hundred yards away so Rich raised his gun and covered the first available opening, which was sixty yards distant. When the big buck hit the opening, Rich blatted with his mouth and stopped the deer. Schweitzer aimed behind the buck's right shoulder and pulled the trigger of his Remington 12-gauge and saw the brute drop in his tracks.

Rich stated that when the buck dropped, he took off running through the multi-flora thorns. When he got to the deer, it started to get back up so a second shot put him down for the count. Yes indeed, something good happened. Something real good had happened. A quick prayer of thanks was lifted up to the Creator.

Rich had just shot a tall tined 18-point buck. If there ever was a whitetail that could be confused with an elk, this would be the deer. The buck's tall sweeping tines resembled a wapiti in many ways. Later on, the buck would be officially measured with a gross score of 192 1/8 Boone and Crockett points and a net score of 172 7/8 non-typical Boone and Crockett points. Schweitzer immediately called Charlie and said, "You've got to get up here. I've just shot the kind of monster buck that we've been trying to get for all of these years!"

A second call was placed to Rich's brother who was able to leave work and join in the celebration. The three comrades were smart enough to enjoy the moment and take it all in. Throughout the next four days, numerous friends and family came over to share in the occasion.

A few months later, Rich shared his story with me and stated, "The fun for me is that I shot him on my own land that I created and maintained for deer hunting. It's not about the kill; it's about sharing time in the woods with good friends. The real memories are in sharing it with people that I care about."

Something real good happened, friends developed a stronger bond and a pleasant lifetime memory was created. Camaraderie, a welcome side effect to the deer hunting lifestyle!

Meat Eater

"And God said, Let us make man in our image, after our likeness; and let them have dominion over the fish of the sea and over the fowl of the air, and over the cattle and over all the earth and over every creeping thing that creepeth upon the earth." **Genesis 1:26**

"Every moving thing that lives shall be food for you. And as I gave you the green plants, I give you everything." **Genesis 9:3**

"Now then, take your weapons, your quiver and your bow and go out to the field and hunt game for me." **Genesis 27:3**

A lot of titles are placed on people throughout the course of their lives. Mine would include son, brother, husband, step-father, athlete, hunter, writer, author,

Christian, etc. Another title that strongly defines me is *meat-eater*. I for one am so thankful to be created in God's own image and given dominion over all of the food sources created for our benefit. If you have made it this far into the book, then you obviously know that hunting is a strong part of who I am and that I absolutely love to eat meat. For me, a meal is incomplete if it does not contain some form of meat. There is nothing finer than sitting down for a meal of grilled salmon, fried perch, fire-roasted trout, fresh venison tenderloins, or marinated steak skewers. During my single days, I would often grill up an extra-large steak and eat it with just a glass of milk!

On a Thursday night in February of 2012, my wife, Michelle, informed me that she and the kids were attending a school auction meeting at another parent's house and that I was on my own for dinner. I reverted back to my bachelor days and grilled an extra-large, thick sirloin steak to the highly desirable medium-rare condition and then commenced to feast on the beast. When I was about three fourths of the way done, I suddenly felt a burning sensation in my chest. My throat started filling up with saliva and I bee-lined it to the sink in an attempt to *cough up* the meat that was now caught deep within my chest. I struggled for a solid forty-five minutes before deciding that I had better call my wife and ask her to come home in case I passed out. On her way home, she called one of her best friends, Donna, who is a registered nurse and asked her to meet us at our house.

My ordeal started at 5:20 p.m. Michelle and Donna talked me into going to the Emergency room at 7 p.m. Xrays at the hospital revealed that I had a piece of steak lodged in my esophagus and a doctor was called in to remove the obstruction with a procedure that I was told would last approximately twenty minutes. When I finally went under anesthesia, it was 9:30 p.m.

Unbeknownst to me, the *simple* procedure did not go as planned. The doctor was unable to dislodge and/or remove the meat after several attempts and gave up, fearing that further attempts would cause damage to my now-bruised esophagus. Instead, they hooked me up to a ventilator, kept me medically sedated and housed me in the Critical Care Unit. Several hours later, Michelle and my mom were able to see me, and what they saw was not pretty. They watched as several medical staff physically restrained me as I came out of the anesthesia and freaked out from having a tube stuck deep down into my throat.

On Friday morning, my mother called my five younger siblings and informed them of my current situation. They found this news to be quite alarming since they were told the night before that I was to have a quick out-patient procedure and would be back to normal.

Friday was a long day for my family as I lay unconscious on life support with the meat still lodged in my throat. Saturday arrived and the various doctors consulted and held differing opinions. The surgeon wanted to wait until Sunday to try again but the other doctors as well as my family, all pushed to have the procedure sooner (Saturday) than later (Sunday). The surgeon finally complied and attempted the procedure Saturday evening. This time the doctor lassoed the meat cutting it in half and the two pieces fell harmlessly into my stomach.

Later that night, I semi-awoke for a long enough period to realize that I had a room full of visitors. I then dozed off until early Sunday morning, awoke and waited for Michelle to return and spring me loose. I wanted to go home.

Michelle and the kids entered my room around 8 a.m. I was glad that the kids came to see me, but I didn't think that it was good for them to miss school so I asked Michelle, "Why aren't the kids in school?"

She looked at me and said, "There is no school, it is Sunday."

My mind could not comprehend what she was telling me; it just didn't make sense so I responded, "It's Friday."

Michelle shook her head and repeated, "No, it's Sunday. You have been here for a couple of days."

To lose two complete days over what should have been a quick simple procedure was quite alarming. As the nurses weaned me off the medication, I remembered a few events that occurred when I popped in and out of consciousness.

I remembered awakening from the anesthesia and feeling the ventilator tube stuck down my throat. For some reason, fear overtook me and I felt scared. I tried to take the tube out and found myself fighting with numerous medical personnel. I entered the hospital at six feet one inch, two hundred and twenty five pounds and a male nurse told Michelle that I gave them quite a fight until they were able to increase the dosage on one of the numerous I.Vs, which then returned me to la-la land.

As I said earlier, I knew nothing about my ordeal until early Sunday morning. Unfortunately, there were side effects to being on the ventilator as long as I was. It took quite a while for my lungs to recover. Much to my dismay, I wasn't released until Tuesday night. When I was finally discharged, I had a full beard and hair on what is usually, my shaved head.

Recovery took a lot longer than I expected. Just walking from the bedroom to the living room made me winded. My lung capacity was low, and I had to do breathing exercises to build it back up. It took two full weeks before I could even stand for ten minutes or more. Eventually my full strength returned, and I am extremely thankful to be alive and well. This whole ordeal revealed to me how precious our time is here on earth. Our lives can be drastically changed in a blink of an eye.

Hunting and eating meat both give me great pleasure, and I am glad that the two activities walk hand in hand. My quality of life is greatly enriched with the adventurous pursuit of wild game and the utilization of this great resource. Non-hunters will often irrationally plea, "Why don't you give the deer guns so they can fight back." Well, in this particular case, a cow fought back – not an animal that I killed but nevertheless it was indeed killed for my eating pleasure.

My health scare enhanced my appreciation for the gift of life. I thank God for every precious second. Now that I am once again living strong and in good health, I want to further maximize my time on earth and live in accordance with God's design as outlined in His story of creation, which is found in the book of Genesis. God created us in His image and gave us dominion over the earth and all the creatures upon it. I look forward to many more exciting hunting adventures and many more delicious meals of meat. Glory to God!

In everything give thanks: for this is the will of God in Christ Jesus concerning you.

1 Thessalonians 5:18

So whether you eat or drink or whatever you do, do it all for the glory of God.

1 Corinthians 10:31

Gifted

Christmas Eve is the ultimate experience for a child growing up with a strong family structure in the United States. The anticipation of what the following morning will produce invokes sleepless nights and early morning wake ups.

Looking under the tree and seeing a long narrow shaped package gets the young outdoorsman hoping in earnest that the unwrapping will produce the desired gun needed for hunting adventures. Hunting stories shared by my dad and his friends combined with the many stories that I read in various hunting magazines had me eagerly hoping for the gift of a gun.

Sure enough, my parents didn't disappointment me. My Christmas morning gun was tucked safely into a suede leather case that possessed a sheep skin lining. When I unzipped that beautiful case, I was greeted with a 12-gauge Ithaca Deer Slayer shotgun.

I used that gun to shoot quite a few deer but another important gift was equally important. My dad gifted his time and introduced me to the wonderful wild world of hunting.

Later in life, my dad complained about his feet always being cold so I was able to repay him by buying him a pair of warm pack boots that he unwrapped one Christmas morning. I also had the privilege of pushing deer to him as he stood ready in ambush. Hearing gunfire coming from the direction of my dad after a successful *push* is still one of my favorite hunting memories. On one occasion, I was pushing a shrub-infested thicket and could see my dad posted up on a ridge in the distance. On that hunt, I not only heard the gun fire but watched the flames leap from his gun barrel as he shot a 6-point buck that was fleeing from my encroachment into his territory.

Like a well-bred hunting dog, hunting has gotten into my blood and helps define who I am. I have now developed proficient skills and enjoy many successful outings. In southern Michigan, we can often harvest more than one deer and I have been able to gift others with venison. Some of the recipients have included single mothers who appreciated the food because of their current limited income. Another regular recipient has been a friend of the family who has health issues and cannot eat processed foods or store bought meats. I highly doubt that any of these non-hunters will vote against hunting when the anti-hunting movement fights to get various anti-hunting causes on the ballot.

The Bible states, "Give and it will be given to you. A loud measure, pressed down, shaken together and running over will be poured into your lap. For with the measure you use, it will be measured to you," Luke 6:38. We do not give for the purpose of receiving but as the Bible says, those who do give are most often rewarded.

My brother, Jeff, and his neighbor, Dick, were gifted the opportunity of hunting elk in Colorado. Both Jeff and Dick had performed various acts of charity for their neighbor. Since the neighbor's father lived hundreds of miles away, he wanted to repay their kindness with a hunt. Jeff and Dick took him up on his offer and stayed at the man's spacious log home.

This gentleman was a lifetime bowhunter. He had treestands strategically posted on elk trails to ambush the animals as they made their way back down the mountain to the fields at night. On the fourth night, Jeff saw a five by five bull advancing towards him. Even though Jeff was positioned thirty feet up an aspen tree, he was level with the bull when it stepped into a shooting lane twenty yards away. A perfectly placed shot at the broadside animal resulted in a quick recovery. Jeff got to fulfill a lifetime dream because of the twofold act of giving.

Just like my earthly father gifted me his time and resources to hunt, I personally believe that my heavenly Father gifted mankind *the hunting spirit.* Through hunting, we have a front row seat to God's creation. My first-hand observations of nature reinforce my belief in God. The Creator of life communicates to us through His handiwork, His loving spirit and his word, the Bible. I used to wonder why ultimate predators like grizzly bears feared man when they can obviously overpower humans in a physical match-up. Genesis 9:2 tells us that God put the fear of man into all beasts of the earth, sky and sea. After the great flood, God speaks to Noah. "The fear and dread of you (man) will fall on all of the beasts of the earth, and on all the birds in the sky, on every creature that moves along the ground, and on all the fish in the sea; they are given into your hands. Everything that lives and moves about will be food for you. Just as I give you the green plants, I now give you everything," Genesis 9:2&3.

The hunting spirit has been gifted to you. Happy Hunting!

Acknowledgements

I wish to acknowledge and extend my heartfelt gratitude to the following people for their prominent contributions towards the development of *The Hunting Spirit*. I am thankful that Connie Crofoot (editor) and Sharie Schnell (cover graphics) extended their time and talents in providing their valuable services. In addition, I want to thank Greg McElveen of Big Mac Publishers for publishing my second book!

I would also like to thank the following people for sharing their personal hunting stories with me. This group includes: Jeff Lambert, Joe Lambert, Glen Roberts, Marla Roberts, Jessica Olmstead, Rick Dosh, Guy Picketts Jr., Robert Reits, Joe Alongi, Joel Ruggles, Rob Miller, Mike Riepen, Rich Schweitzer, Tony Snyder and Rick Grosteffon. In addition, I wish to extend my gratitude to Mike Persichini for allowing me to use his outstanding photographs which are included in the chapters *Bartholomew* and *I Believe in Monsters* and David Kenyon for providing me with the bear photograph for the chapter *Randy's Bear-Cleansing Ritual*.

Michelle Lambert, my wonderful wife, this book would not be possible without your love and support and for that I am extremely thankful. I also want to thank God Almighty, the Creator, for gifting me with *The Hunting Spirit*. It is my prayer that this book touches many lives and that *His Spirit* shines through!

About the Author

Jerry Lambert is the author of *Trophy White Tales: A classic collection of campfire stories about North America's #1 game animal – the whitetail deer*, an Amazon Best Seller in the Hunting category. Jerry is also a free-lance outdoor writer who has been published in *Bear Hunting, Big Buck, Buck Fax, Michigan Out-of-Doors, Michigan Outdoor News, mossyoak.com, North American Whitetail, Turkey Country* and *Woods-N-Water News*. In addition, he is a life member of the National Rifle Association. To learn more about the author, visit his website *jerrylambertoutdoors.com,* or *The Hunting Spirit* Facebook page.

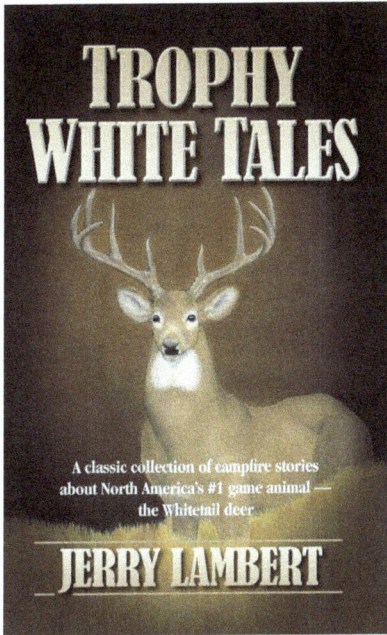

"What a wonderful book! Anybody who appreciates the sights, sounds and smells of God's creation will enjoy this book. These are stories that the everyday hunter will relate to and enjoy." **Greg Abbas, host of A-Way Outdoors Television.**

"Trophy White Tales is a great book, from a great writer. The stories are short, from two to five pages each, and it is easy to pick up, read one or two, and look forward to picking it up the next time. In all, great tales, well told." *Jeff Davis, editor of Whitetails Unlimited.*

"Jerry does a great job of conveying the mystery and the suspense that a morning in the woods can offer. By weaving tall tales and personal stories together, he gives the reader a sense of the lure of opening day, the anticipation of the hunt and the spiritual sense the woods has to offer." **Jimmy Gretzinger, host of** *Michigan Out-of-Doors* **television show.**

"Trophy White Tales is more than a book about harvesting deer. It is a map of one man's life journey as he experiences the fraternity of a deer camp, searches for a ghost buck, builds lasting memories with his father and brothers, and catches the infamous buck fever on more than one occasion. Jerry Lambert joins the circle of effective storytellers who keep the pages turning in the hands of the reader. He is a good hunter and a good writer. I personally enjoyed every tale - whether a tall one or not. I highly recommend this book!" **Dr. Jimmy Sites, Producer/Host:** *Spiritual Outdoor Adventures TV.*

"Trophy White Tales is a refreshing conglomerate of anecdotal and personal short stories that every whitetail hunter can enjoy! Jerry Lambert delivers the campfire to his readers in the most quintessence form. A warm blend of family values and situations everyone who has hunted deer can relate to is enthusiastically and sometimes impishly told by the author. Place your name in any of the short stories and undoubtedly you'll think the story was written about you." **Marc Anthony, Outdoor Writer, deer hunter with five Boone & Crockett bucks.**

"Jerry really brings you into the woods on all his adventures and makes you feel like you are there with him. **Tim Hart,** *Q1 Buck Pole Television* **host.**

"Trophy White Tales is a great compilation of stories that we can all relate to. A wonderful fireside book for all ages. You will be captivated by the lore of yesteryear and a better sportsman by the tips given. Now, grab a cup of coffee and throw another log on the fire and enjoy! **Dave Wilkins,** *Droptine Outdoor Adventures,* **Owner.**

"Jerry brings out some of the best hunting stories ever told in his latest title, "Trophy White Tales." His focus on the whitetail deer with an emphasis on Michigan makes this book a must read for every typical mid-west hunter. His focus on family and credit to God makes the experiences told in this book even more essential as we pass the experience of hunting the whitetail deer on to the following generations." **Calvin Beeke,** *Michigan Whitetail Pursuit*

"He's (author) an excellent storyteller - in the same tree-stand as the likes of Garrison Keillor, Paul Harvey and Ernie Harwell - and you find yourself melting into the scenes he describes." **Will Kowalski,** *Battle Creek Enquire*r

"This is a volume that not only belongs on your outdoors bookshelf to read and reread in and out of deer season, but a second copy also should be kept at deer camp. It will certainly be in demand." **Betty Sodders, Outdoor Writer.**

"In Jerry's book you get all kinds of fun, thrilling and intense stories of his outdoor experiences. These take place all over this great country. Great tree stand book. Get the WEI and Games away from your kids and get this book in their hands. Then go outside and enjoy God's gift to all men – His Creation. **Rocky McElveen, Author of** *Wild Men, Wild Alaska* **&** *Wild Men, Wild Alaska 2.*

"A must have for every hunter. If you're looking for a book to help you get geared up for hunting season, make sure you purchase this one." **Lane Walker, Author of** *Hometown Hunter Series.*

www.ingramcontent.com/pod-product-compliance
Lightning Source LLC
LaVergne TN
LVHW050624090426
835512LV00007B/658